CPUnleashed!
Tapping Processor Speed

by D. James Benton

Copyright © 2022 by D. James Benton, all rights reserved.

Preface

Even as processors get faster, applications get slower. Why? Inefficient software. There was a time when every BYTE and every FLOP mattered, because resources and speed were so limited. As processors have greatly improved, diligence has been cast aside like an old shoe. It is high time we brought back diligence, unleashed the CPU, and tapped into processor speed. In this text we explore what makes applications slow, how to avoid bottlenecks, and optimize utilization of these amazing chips. While this text deals specifically with Intel™ processors, the principles apply to all modern ones. By necessity, we will be focusing on machine language and code; so get ready for some assembler. Our purpose here is to crunch numbers as rapidly as possible with readily available hardware.

All of the examples contained in this book,
(as well as a lot of free programs) are available at...
https://www.dudleybenton.altervista.org/software/index.html

Figure 1. Intel™ 7th Gen Processors

Figure 2. Intel™ CPU Cooling Fan for i3 i5 i7

Table of Contents

	page
Preface	i
Chapter 1. Don't Pull the Fire Alarm to Deliver a Pizza	1
Chapter 2. Instructions Are Not All Equal	3
Chapter 3. Absolute Value as an Example	5
Chapter 4. Vector Instruction Set	11
Chapter 5. Polynomials and Horner's Method	15
Chapter 6. Pivoting	17
Chapter 7. Computationally Intensive Functions	21
Chapter 8. Computationally Intensive Procedures	27
Chapter 9. Basic Matrix Operations	37
Chapter 10. Advanced Matrix Operations	43
Chapter 11. Banded Matrix Solutions	49
Chapter 12. Avoiding a Brute Force Approach	59
Chapter 13. Fast Fourier Transform	69
Chapter 14. Romberg vs. Gauss	75
Chapter 15. Predictor/Corrector vs. Runge-Kutta	79
Chapter 16. Implicit vs. Explicit Methods	85
Appendix A. Instructions	95
Appendix B. Registers	101
Appendix C. The FPU	103
Appendix D. Steam Properties in Assembler	105
Appendix E. Moist Air Properties in Assembler	107
Appendix F. Procedure Level Timing	109
Appendix G. Speed Test	111

Figure 3. Intel™ i287 FPU

Figure 4. Intel™ i387/i487 FPUs

Chapter 1. Don't Pull the Fire Alarm to Deliver a Pizza

The first programming atrocity we will consider is: *throwing an exception*. Whether you intend for it to happen or are even aware of it happening in your code or some borrowed code that you are utilizing, this action is often invoked in object-oriented code. One common example is encountering an uninitialized pointer (address to a location in memory). Throwing an exception serves to allocate some block of memory and perhaps initialize the contents. The initialization process may encounter yet another uninitialized pointer and so on, resulting in an explosion of exceptions, each one pending completion of the ones descendant from it. While we could implement such a sequence of instructions on an Intel™8086, it would quickly overrun the stack and lock up the processor. More recent processors with much greater memory can handle this ridiculous waste of resources but that doesn't mean it's a smart or efficient thing to do.

Throwing an exception is like pulling the fire alarm. While the pizza place might be right next door to the firehouse, dispatching a team of firefighters in the big red truck to deliver a pizza is an absurd waste of resources. Exceptions (which are a special type of processor instruction) should be reserved for catastrophes, not routine. Dividing by zero and over- or under-running an array, these are events worthy of throwing an exception. Allocating your silly array that should have been properly and explicitly managed is not worthy of pulling the fire alarm.

Throwing an exception initiates a whole sequence of other events, including: interrupting the operating system and saving all of the processor variables and state flags so that it can later pick up where it left off. This is very much like herding all the children out of the classrooms and into the parking lot, then taking roll to make sure none have been left in what might be a burning building. This is so very much more wasteful than having one child raise their hand, wait for the teacher to notice them, and asking to go to the restroom without disrupting the classroom or the entire school.

Why does this happen? Ignorance and laziness! Ignorance, in that the programmers who utilize this method of allocating and initializing variables and code probably have no idea just how costly it is. Laziness in that those programmers who might understand the cost to the processor, take the easy path for themselves because it's just a few keys away.

The bottom line? Don't do it and don't incorporate other's code that does. How do you make sure? See to it that you explicitly define, allocate, and initialize every single variable. This doesn't mean that only static variables can be used, only that every step is explicitly encoded and none rely on the processor bursting into flames when encountering a piece of your code. A few instructions may suffice if you are tidy rather than thousands of instructions the sloppy way.

Chapter 2. Instructions Are Not All Equal

While some earlier processors might have performed one instruction per clock tick or required the same amount of time to process any one of many instructions, this is not true for Intel™ processors. It matters which instructions you use to accomplish a task. What's more, all recent Intel™ processors have a pre-processor that helps funnel tasks into the main processor. Having a pre-processor can greatly speed the time required to accomplish a given task. Causing the pre-processor to *stumble* or kick out of a repetitive pattern can result in a greater delay than would occur had the pre-processor done nothing to facilitate the flow of data and tasks. If you don't understand what the processor and pre-processor are doing, how they work together, and how your code or compiler options influence this, then you will never be able to optimize the performance of your application.

Ultimately, if you ever hope to understand code optimization, you must understand machine language, that is assembler, the instructions that the chip actually processes. You must dig deeper than some high-level script. You must get inside each function, each equation, and each loop. You must learn how the high-level code (e.g., C, FORTRAN, Pascal) is translated by the compiler into machine language. It is not necessary to learn that PUSH BX is 0x53 because the compiler or assembler will handle this for you. You do, however, need to know that the following loop:

```
int i,n;
for(n=i=0;i<8;i++)
   n+=i;
```

when compiled into assembler becomes:

```
1       MOV DWORD PTR i,0
2       MOV EAX,i
3       MOV n,EAX
4       JMP L2
5  L1:  MOV ECX,i
6       ADD ECX,1
7       MOV i,ECX
8  L2:  CMP i,8
9       JGE L3
10      MOV EDX,n
11      ADD EDX,i
12      MOV n,EDX
13      JMP L1
14 L3:
```

The first statement sets i to zero and the processor must be told that i is a double WORD (32-bit) integer. The second instruction sets the DWORD register EAX equal to i. The third instruction puts this same value (zero) into the variable n, which is also a DWORD. The fourth instruction jumps over the increment code (this is the way the C compiler implements loops). The fifth instruction moves i into the register ECX and requires a label (L1), as we will jump back to this location from the bottom of the loop. The sixth instruction adds 1 to ECX. We could accomplish this same thing with INC ECX but the compiler uses this encoding, as it works for increments other than 1 and simplifies the compilers task, if not that of the processor. The seventh instruction copies the incremented value (ECX) back into i. We could accomplish this same thing with INC DWORD PTR[i], where [i] is the address of i, but this too is simpler for the compiler, if not the processor.

The eighth instruction compares i to the loop end value of 8 and requires a label (L2), as we jump to this location from the start. The ninth instruction is a conditional jump (if greater than or equal to), which kicks control out of the loop to location L3. The tenth instruction moves n into EDX. The eleventh instruction adds i to EDX. The twelfth instruction saves this value in n. The thirteenth instruction jumps back to the top of the loop.

This implementation of the two-line C loop is rather inefficient, though typical of what compliers achieve. A more streamlined and faster implementation would be:

```
1       MOV EAX,0
2       MOV EDX,0
3       MOV ECX,8
4 L1:   INC EAX
5       ADD EDX,EAX
6       LOOP L1
7       MOV n,EDX
```

Sometimes an optimizing compiler can achieve an even better sequence than we might come up with, but often it won't and that's what makes the difference and how we will tap into the speed of these wonderful processors.

Chapter 3. Absolute Value as an Example

To begin our discussion of the particulars of how coding impacts speed, we start with the example of taking the absolute value of a vector (linear array) of floating-point numbers. We will often refer to a contiguous group of floating-point numbers as a *vector*, which might be a one-dimensional array or multi-dimensional. A common example of a square (n×n) two-dimensional array would be a matrix, which we will discuss solving in subsequent chapters.

There are at least four ways of tackling this problem, spanning a considerable range of speeds. Perhaps the most common is also the slowest and can be represented by the following code snippet:

```
for(i=0;i<n;i++)
   x[i]=fabs(x[i]);
```

We can see how Visual Studio™ implements this by activating the assembler output with the /Fa compiler option:

```
 1    MOV   DWORD PTR i,0
 2    JMP   L2
 3 L1:MOV   EAX,DWORD PTR i
 4    ADD   EAX,1
 5    MOV   DWORD PTR i,EAX
 6 L2:CMP   EAX,n
 7    JGE   L3
 8    MOV   ECX,DWORD PTR i
 9    PUSH  QWORD PTR x[ECX*8]
10    CALL  _fabs
11    ADD   ESP,8
12    FSTP  QWORD PTR x[ECX*8]
13    JMP   L1
14 L3:
```

We see in lines 1-7 and 13-14 above, the same loop implementation as in the first code snippet in Chapter 2. This begins with setting the loop index (i) to one and jumping over the increment count, comparing this to the end (n) and kicking out of the loop to L3. Next we push the QWORD (64-bit floating-point) value of x[i] onto the processor (not the FPU) stack and calling the function _fabs(). The address of x[i] is equal to the bottom of x plus 8×i, where i is stored in ECX so that we get x[ECX*8], which will be converted to a simple absolute address by the pre-processor so the *8 doesn't add any appreciable execution time. This, of course, would not be true for an 8086, which couldn't accept the instruction [ECX*8] and, in fact, wouldn't accept an address with CX in it.

The library function fabs() expects a single 64-bit (8 BYTE or QWORD) floating-point operand pushed onto the CPU (not FPU) stack. It takes the absolute value using the FABS instruction and leaves the result on the FPU stack. This exiting convention is true for all functions returning a single floating-point value (whether single-precision 32-bit or double-precision 64-bit). This same sort of convention is true for functions returning a single integer value. 64-bit integer return values are expected to be in RAX, 32-bit integer return values are expected to be in the EAX register, 16-bit integer return values are expected to be in the AX register, and 8-bit integer return values are expected to be in the AL register. This is true for signed or unsigned integers. When operating in 16-bit mode, 32-bit integer return values are expected to be split between two registers: the low part in AX and the high part in DX.

This first (and slowest) implementation of this task not only has an explicit (and rather inefficient) loop, but also includes a function call that pushes values onto both the CPU and FPU stacks and then must pop off both as well. The CPU stack is utilized on the way in and the FPU stack is utilized on the way out. Inside the fabs() function, information is retrieved from the CPU stack and then loaded onto the FPU stack. The entire process is inefficient. While it may not take an inordinate amount of time for a small example, details like this matter when you are solving huge arrays or even ones of modest size many times.

The next implementation we will consider is shown in this next code snippet:

```
for(i=0;i<n;i++)
   if(x[i]<0.)
      x[i]=-x[i];
```

While this might not seem like much of an improvement and requires 3 lines of code rather than 2, we have eliminated the function call with its overhead.

When compiled into assembler, these three lines of C become:

```
 1   MOV   DWORD PTR i,0
 2   JMP   L2
 3L1:MOV   EAX,DWORD PTR i
 4   ADD   EAX,1
 5   MOV   DWORD PTR i,EAX
 6L2:CMP   EAX,n
 7   JGE   L3
 8   MOV   ECX,DWORD PTR i
 9   LEA   EDX,x
10   FLDZ
11   FCOM  QWORD PTR[EDX+ECX*8]
12   FNSTSW AX
13   TEXT  AH,0x65
14   JNE   L1
15   FLD QWORD PTR[EDX+ECX*8]
16   FCHS
17   FSTP QWORD PTR[EDX+ECX*8]
18   JMP L1
19L3:
```

The looping part is the same as before. Instead of calling the fabs() function, the comparison and conditional sign change is handled locally. In order to compare x[i] to 0.0, we must first load 0.0 onto the FPU stack with the FLDZ instruction. The comparison is accomplished with the FCOM instruction. The flags on the FPU have been set, but these are not directly accessible to the CPU, so we must get the status word to the CPU using the FNSTSW instruction. The various conditions indicated by the FPU flags can be found in the Intel™ manual. The one we are interested in here is hex 65. If this is not true (x is not less than zero) then we go on to the next index. If it is true, then we must load x[i] onto the stack, change the sign with the FCHS instruction, and pop it back off the FPU stack and into x[i]. The pre-processor handles the [EDX+ECX*8], converting it to an absolute offset.

While the second implementation without the function call is often faster, this is not always the case for every compilation and processor combination. The switch back-and-forth between CPU and FPU instructions plus the conditional jumps can cause the pre-processor to stumble so that the second implementation may be slower than the first. If you are unaware of the pre-processor's participation in this process, the outcome of speed comparison tests may seem counterintuitive or even meaningless.

The third implementation we consider is the simplest possible loop with the fewest possible tests and jumps. This minimal loop can be implemented using inline assembler within C code as follows:

```
__asm
{
MOV    ECX,N
LEA    EAX,x
L1:FLD QWORD PTR[EAX]
   FABS
   FSTP QWORD PTR[EAX]
   ADD  EAX,8
   LOOP L1
}
```

which is equivalent to:

```
1    MOV    ECX,N
2    LEA    EAX,x
3 L1:FLD QWORD PTR[EAX]
4    FABS
5    FSTP QWORD PTR[EAX]
6    ADD  EAX,8
7    LOOP L1
```

We load the loop number (n) into ECX (the loop register) and the offset of x[0] into EAX using the LEA (load effective address) instruction. The looping begins at L1, where we load x[i] onto the FPU, take the absolute value using the FABS instruction, and pop the result off back into x[i]. Then we add 8 (as these are 8-BYTE or 64-bit floating-point values). The LOOP instruction repeats these steps ECX times. We never even need the index i, as we use EAX for this. Another benefit is that there is no implicit test (FCOM) and no repetitive loading of 0.0 (FLDZ) and no conditional jump statements to trip up the pre-processor. In fact, the pre-processor won't do anything to this code before passing it along, which will be faster most of the time.

The fourth implementation takes advantage of the difference between integer and floating-point number formats. With integers, -1 is the number that if you add 1 to it becomes zero. This is not the sign bit followed by zeroes. Instead, it's all 1s in binary. For example in 8-bits binary notation -1=11111111 because when you add 1 to it becomes 10000000. Only the last 8 bits remain, while the 9th bit (1) becomes the overflow flag. In hexadecimal notation, -1=0xFF. This is not true for the IEEE-754 floating-point standard on which the Intel™ FPU is based. There is a sign bit. Because there is an actual sign bit, we can simply check and modify a single bit to accomplish this task (fabs) and never involve the FPU. The same is true for swapping the sign of a floating-point number (x=-x). We can perform the entire loop in C using a logical AND (&) with a BYTE or QWORD pointer or in a very simple assembler loop. Implementation in C would be:

```
for(i=0;i<n;i++)
   (__int64)x[i]&=0x7FFFFFFF;
```

The location x[i] is explicitly converted to an unsigned QWORD (or __int64) and the high sign bit is cleared by the logical AND (& in C) operation. With the Pentium™ and later processors it doesn't matter (for speed) if a QWORD or BYTE operation is performed. With earlier processors, it would be marginally faster to only modify the BYTE containing the sign bit. This would necessitate shifting the pointer by 7 BYTES and using 0x7F. We could accomplish this quickly with the following code, which could be inserted into C using the __asm qualifier:

```
1     MOV ECX,N
2     LEA EDI,x
3     ADD EDI,7
4     MOV AL,0x7F
5 L1: AND ES:EDI,AL
6     ADD EDI,8
7     LOOP L1
```

Again ECX is used for the loop counter (1 to n) and i is not needed. Here we use LEA to load the effective address of the array x[] along with EDI (the destination index). We add 7 to arrive at the BYTE containing the sign bit. We use AL (a BYTE register) to store the value for the logical AND. We don't need to specify a size for the AND instruction because AL implicitly controls this detail. We increment the destination index by 8 for each of the double-precision (64-bit) floating-point variables in the array x[].

We could use these same instructions with only slight modifications with single-precision (32-bit) floating-point values (e.g., changing QWORD to DWORD and *8 or ADD 8 to *4 or ADD 4). While there are other differences between single- and double-precision floating-point values (including number of significant digits in the mantissa and bits associated with the exponent), the sign bit is in the same location. There was a time before FPUs were prevalent or part of the CPU chip when single-precision floating-point calculations were common. With the introduction (and now ubiquitous) presence of FPUs, this is no longer the case. In fact, as the Intel™ FPUs work with 80-bit floating-point values natively, it is slower to operate with 32-bit values.

More Sign Operations

Just as the sign bit can be *cleared* using AND 0x7F, it can be *set* using OR 0x80 and also *reversed* (inverted) using XOR 0x80. The same code can be used to perform any of these operations.

Chapter 4. Vector Instruction Set

It is not practical to customize every single line of code in a lengthy model. It is much more efficient to identify those few intense calculation loops that dominate the runtime. Which these are is not always obvious but we shall discuss this in Chapter 7. We will first introduce the concept of a Vector Instruction Set (VIS) that can easily be called and which will quickly perform repetitive tasks involving arrays or polynomials. We will discuss polynomials in Chapter 5.

In 1980 when I began working at TVA, we had a Hewlett-Packard (HP) minicomputer the size of a refrigerator. While this in-house resource did allow us to accomplish many things, it was inadequate for some tasks, including the transient reservoir and climate models, which were used to manage and optimize TVA's system of dams and hydroelectric plants. These models required a mainframe computer. TVA had several of these of the IBM (International Business Machines) variety, mostly for business applications.

For scientific applications, the CDC (Control Data Corporation) mainframes were preferred over the IBM. Furthermore, CDC also had a line called STAR, which were *vector* processors. These specialized mainframes could process arrays of floating-point numbers much more rapidly than the *scalar* processors at the time. We had an account on the CDC STAR and a terminal locally. This is how the big models were run at the TVA Engineering Laboratory from 1978 through 1982.

This practice (running big models on the CDC vector processor mainframe) was in effect when I joined the Team in 1980. Many of the modeling codes (all written in FORTRAN) had been rewritten to take advantage of vector processing when I arrived. I subsequently converted several more. This practice continued for approximately 4 years when a new (and much cheaper in-house) option materialized.

New optional hardware for the HP minicomputer became available, including vector processing. This new option consisted of additional circuit boards that only performed a single operation (e.g., floating-point add), but did so at a significantly faster pace than the main FPU. In order to access this added hardware, there was also a special set of functions (called vector instruction set or VIS). The software had to be modified to migrate from the CDC approach to HP's approach for tapping into this extra speed, but the conversion was not burdensome and soon we had all the models running on the in-house equipment and dropped the CDC contract.

This approach was so successful that we converted even more software to take advantage of this new hardware and became quite dependent on the speed and convenience it afforded. I even adapted the steam properties to vector implementation. These particular calculations were a considerable burden at the time for newly-emerging power plant modeling software. All was going well...

From 1983 and into 1984, the TVA Engineering Laboratory computer modeling teams began shifting hardware once again, this time from the HP minicomputer to PCs and microcomputers. While other groups within the organization began the shift earlier, it wasn't practical for our Team until FPUs were readily available. Once the transition began, the burden of maintaining minicomputers drove the process forward.

I originally wrote a code-level compatibility equivalent of the HP VIS for Microsoft™ and Intel™ that required no modification of the models. While implementing this, I realized that a speed increase was also possible with the new hardware, provided the VIS was properly encoded in assembler. That is how my VIS came into being. The instructions in my VIS along with their relative advantage are listed in the following table for an Intel™ Centrino™.

Table 4.1 VIS Speeds

```
         FLOATING POINT OPERATION SPEED - ALL VALUES ARE IN KFLOPS
single precision operations                          scalar  vector speed
kernel   function   [16,128,1024 is the length]      speed  16  128  1024
VABS     abs val    (V2(I)=ABS(V1(I)),I=1,N)          109   14  112   895
VADD     add        (V3(I)=V1(I)+V2(I),I=1,N)         112   14  112   895
VCLA     clamp      (V(I)=VMIN≤V(I)≤VMAX,I=1,N)       224   28  224  1790
VDIV     divide     (V3(I)=V1(I)/V2(I),I=1,N)         112   14  112   895
VDOT     dot prod   S=SUM(V1(I)*V2(I),I=1,N)          112   14  112   895
VMAB     max abs    V(M)=MAX(ABS(V(I)),I=1,N)         112   14  112   895
VMAX     maximum    V(M)=MAX(V(I),I=1,N)              112   14  112   895
VMIB     min abs    V(M)=MIN(ABS(V(I)),I=1,N)         112   14  112   895
VMIN     minimum    V(M)=MIN(V(I),I=1,N)              112   14  112   895
VMOV     move       (V2(I)=V1(I),I=1,N)               112   14  112   895
VMPY     multiply   (V3(I)=V1(I)*V2(I),I=1,N)         112   14  112   895
VNRM     norm       S=SUM(ABS(V1(I)),I=1,N)           112   14  112   895
VPOL     polynomial P=SUM(C(I)*X**(I-1),I=1,N)        224   28  224  1790
VPIV     pivot      (V3(I)=S*V1(I)+V2(I),I=1,N)       224   28  224  1790
VSAD     add        (V2(I)=S+V1(I),I=1,N)             112   14  112   895
VSDV     divide     (V2(I)=S/V1(I),I=1,N)             112   14  112   895
VSMY     multiply   (V2(I)=S*V1(I),I=1,N)             112   14  112   895
VSSB     subtract   (V2(I)=S-V1(I),I=1,N)             112   14  112   895
VSUB     subtract   (V3(I)=V1(I)-V2(I),I=1,N)         112   14  112   895
VSUM     sum        S=SUM(V1(I),I=1,N)                112   14  112   895
VSWP     swap       (V1(I)<->V2(I),I=1,N)             112   14  112   895
VMIX     index mov  (V2(I)=V1(INDEX(I)),I=1,N)        112   14  112   895
VMXI     index mov  (V2(INDEX(I))=V1(I),I=1,N)        112   14  112   895
Approximate processor speed=2247 KFLOPS
average scalar speed  =  126 KFLOPS  (typical XT=  5, AT= 16)
average vector speed  =  913 KFLOPS  (typical XT= 19, AT= 42)
average vector advantage = 622%      (typical XT=285, AT=165)
```

The table lists the instruction, it's nominal purpose, a descriptive loop, the scalar speed (ordinary C or FORTRAN code), and the vector speed for length 16, 128, and 1024. Note that there is some setup time (entering and exiting the procedure) so that the longer vector lengths see a greater advantage. All of the speeds are in KFLOPS (1000 floating-point operations per second). Typical speeds for two (now very old) computers (XT and AT models) are also listed for comparison, as these were common when I first put together this table about the time the 80486/80487 was released (circa 1989). At the bottom we see an average speed advantage of the vector over scalar processing of 622%, showing that this approach still has significant value. How else might you achieve a 6× speed increase without purchasing exotic hardware?

The VIS approach means you can compile a program and send it to anyone with a plain vanilla PC and they too will realize a speed increase without changing anything else.

Most of the instructions listed in Table 4.1 will be recognized as common loop tasks, except perhaps the polynomial and pivot. These will be discussed in Chapters 5 and 6, respectively. The first we will discuss here is VABS, which was the focus of Chapter 3. In FORTRAN, we would use the following:

```
CALL VABS(V,I,N)
```

where V is an array of double-precision (64-bit) floating-point reals, I is the step index (1 for every member, 2 for every other member, and so on), and N is the count. Because the HP VIS also included single-precision (32-bit) floating-point instructions and many of the original models used this type, my VIS also includes single-precision equivalents. To distinguish between the two I used VABS4 and VABS8, though these are no longer needed. In C we would use the following:

```
vabs(v,i,n);
```

The scalar implementation of this in FORTRAN would be:

```
SUBROUTINE VABS(V1,I1,N)
DOUBLE PRECISION V1(N)
I1=1
DO J=1,N
  V1(I1)=DABS(V1(I1))
  I1=I1+I
ENDDO
RETURN
END
```

It is necessary to allow for increments other than 1 (I1) because the CDC vector instructions did so, the models were coded with this in mind, and the HP VIS also made provision for this (no doubt inspired by the CDC practice). There is further reason to do this because some matrix operations move row-to-row rather than column-to-column. There are also finite difference equations that involve terms bridging increments other than 1. Many of the TVA reservoir and climate models were multi-dimensional transient FDM codes.

The C implementation for this vector instruction is:
```
void vabs(double v1[],int i1,int n)
  {
  int i,j;
  for(i=j=0;j<n;j++,i+=i1)
    v1[i]=fabs(v1[i]);
  }
```

The complete assembler implementation is:

```
1  VABS  PROC    FAR                    ;begin procedure
2        PUBLIC  _vabs                  ;declare name
3        PUSH    EBP                    ;base pointer
4        MOV     EBP,ESP                ;set frame base
5        PUSH    EDI                    ;save EDI
6        LES     EDI,[EBP+12]           ;get address of n
7        MOV     ECX,ES:[EDI]           ;ECX=n
8        LES     EDI,[EBP+8]            ;get address of i1
9        MOV     EAX,ES:[EDI]           ;EAX=i1
10       SHL     EAX,3                  ;i1*8
11       LES     EDI,[EBP+4]            ;get address of v1
12 VAB1:FLD      QWORD PTR ES:[EDI]     ;load v[i] onto FPU
13       FABS                           ;absolute value
14       FSTP    QWORD PTR ES:[EDI]     ;get abs(v[i]) off FPU
15       ADD     EDI,EAX                ;increment i1*8
16       LOOP    VAB1                   ;loop n times
17       POP     EDI                    ;recover EDI
18       POP     EBP                    ;recover EBP
19       RET                            ;return
20 VABS  ENDP                           ;end procedure
```

Stand-alone procedures are expected to preserve the base pointer (EBP) and also the destination index (EDI) if these are used. This is done by pushing them onto the CPU stack upon entering and popping them off the stack (in reverse order) upon exiting. Every time you push or pop an item the stack pointer (ESP) changes so you must account for line 3 (PUSH EBP) when picking arguments off the stack. In C these are arranged in order of first to last (left to right in the code); whereas, in FORTRAN they are arranged from last to first (right to left in the code). As the pointer (v1) and two integers (i1,n) are all DWORDs in this 32-bit implementation, these arguments will be located at EBP+4, +8, and +12, respectively. In a 64-bit implementation (using RBP etc.) these would be at +8, +16, and +24, respectively. The other VIS instructions are similarly encoded.

Chapter 5. Polynomials and Horner's Method

I have seen the following polynomial expression:

$$p(x) = \sum_{i=0}^{n} C_i x^i \qquad (5.1)$$

implemented in countless codes like this:

```
p=c0+c1*x+c2*x^2+c3*x^3+c4*x^4...
```

While this might work in VBA, in C the ^ operator is a logical XOR and not a power, which leads to the even more inefficient:

```
p=c0+c1*x+c2*pow(x,2)+c3*pow(x,3)+c4*pow(x,4)...;
```

If you are writing programs that contain such things as using the pow() function to calculate integer powers, it's time to stop! Never do this. Instead, use Horner's Method.[1]

```
p=(((c4*x+c3)*x+c2)*x+c1)*x+c0;
```

For some large or arbitrary number of terms, we could implement this same calculation:

```
for(p=c[n-1],i=n-2;i>=0;i--)
    p=p*x+c[i];
```

This calculation is implemented by my VIS instruction VPOL, that was not available in the HP VIS nor on the CDC. Something that might not be immediately evident using Horner's Method with an FPU is the fact several instructions can be eliminated so that an even greater speed increase can be achieved. We don't want to do p=p*x+c. These steps can be implemented by the following assembler:

```
 1     LES   EDI,x                    ;get address of x
 2     FLD   ES:QWORD PTR[EDI]        ;ST(0)=x
 3     MOV   ECX,n                    ;ECX=n
 4     DEC   ECX                      ;ECX=n-1
 5     MOV   EAX,ECX                  ;EAX=n-1
 6     SHL   EAX,3                    ;EAX=(n-1)*8
 7     LES   EDI,c                    ;ES:EDI=c[0]
 8     ADD   EDI,EAX                  ;ES:EDI=c[n-1]
 9     FLD   ES:QWORD PTR[EDI]        ;ST(1)=x;ST(0)=c[n-1]
10 L1: FMUL  ST(1)                    ;ST(0)*=x
11     SUB   EDI,8                    ;ES:EDI=c[i]
12     FADD  ES:QWORD PTR[EDI]        ;ST(0)+=c[i]
13     LOOP  L1                       ;for(i=n-2;i>=0;i--)
14     FSTP  ST(1)                    ;pop FPU stack
```

We first push x onto the FPU stack in ST(0), the top spot. We next load the loop counter (ECX) with n-1 and also use this same to calculate the offset to c[n-1] with a SHL 3 to effect ×8 for the double-precision (64-bit) coefficients,

---

[1] William George Horner (1786–1837) British mathematician and optical physicist

using the destination index (EDI) for this and subsequent values. When we load c[n-1] in step 9, this also pushes x into ST(1). In step 10 we multiply by x, which is in ST(1). We then decrement the pointer to c[i], which is ES:EDI, which we add to ST(1). Step 13 implements the loop n-1 times based on ECX. The last step (14) copies the result from ST(0) to ST(1) and pops the FPU stack, which moves ST(1) back into ST(0), which is where the compilers presume the result will be. The compiler will pop the final result off the FPU stack, returning it to the unloaded state. This calculation can be represented in C by the following instructions:

```
for(p=c[n-1],i=n-2;i>=0;i--)
{
p*=x;
p+=c[i];
}
```

Table 4.1 contains the following entry (along with the header):

kernel	function	[16,128,1024 is the length]	speed	16	128	1024
VPOL	polynomial	P=SUM(C(I)*X**(I-1),I=1,N)		224	28	224	1790

Here we see that for this particular processor (a Centrino™), evaluating a polynomial with 16 terms, the scalar function was faster than the vector by a factor of 8. If the polynomial had 128 terms (rather unlikely), the scalar and vector operations were the same speed. For a polynomial with 1024 terms (highly unlikely) there was an 8× increase in speed. While this sequence of code seems to have little advantage on this particular processor, which has a pre-processor, it reduced the time required to calculate steam properties by a factor of two on earlier processors, making it well worth the effort. There is more discussion of steam property calculations in Appendix D.

Chapter 6. Pivoting

The pivot instruction, listed in Table 4.1 as:

```
kernel   function    [16,128,1024 is the length]  speed  16   128  1024
VPIV     pivot       (V3(I)=S*V1(I)+V2(I),I=1,N)         224   28  224  1790
```

can be expressed in C as:

```
for(i=0;i<n;i++)
    v3[i]=s*v1[i]+v2[i];
```

The purpose of this operation, especially when repetitive, might seem superfluous but it is not. This is exactly what you do many times over in the process known as Gauss-Jordan Elimination[2,3], which is the simplest and most straightforward method for solving simultaneous linear equations in matrix form. It can also be used for other matrix operations, including singular value decomposition, finding eigenvectors and eigenvalues, which we will discuss in Chapter 10. Even with the Centrino™ we see an 8× speed increase for a vector length of 1024, which is not at all unreasonable for a matrix. One example of how we might need to perform these calculations over-and-over again many, many times is solving a transient finite difference or finite element model using the Crank-Nicolson[4,5] technique, which is implicit and, though it is computationally intensive, can provide considerable stability over an explicit method.

We present the 16-bit version of the VPIV code here just to illustrate the differences between the generations of processors and how the code must be modified. If you are accustomed to relying entirely on a FORTRAN or C compiler to produce the correct bitness of machine language code for you, then this will serve as an instructive introduction because this is not true when it comes to assembler, where you must do it all and it is entirely up to you to make it compatible with the rest of the code you plan to use it with.

The following code is crafted to be called by (or linked with) the 16-bit Microsoft™ FORTRAN compiler:

1	VPIV	PROC	FAR	begin procedure
2		PUBLIC	VPIV	declare name
3		PUSH	BP	save base pointer
4		MOV	BP,SP	get stack pointer
5		PUSH	DI	save destination index
6		PUSH	SI	save source index
7		PUSH	DS	save data segment
8		LES	DI,[BP+6]	get address of N

---

[2] Johann Carl Friedrich Gauss (1777–1855) German mathematician and physicist
[3] Wilhelm Jordan (1842-1899) German geodesist and applied mathematician
[4] John Crank (1916–2006) British mathematical physicist, pioneer in the field of partial differential equations
[5] Phyllis Nicolson (1917–1968) British mathematician and physicist

9		MOV	CX,ES:[DI]	set loop counter
10		CMP	CX,0	check for N=0
11		JLE	VPIV2	jump out if N=0
12		LES	DI,[BP+26]	get address of I1
13		MOV	AX,ES:[DI]	AX=I1
14		SAL	AX,1	AX=I1*2
15		SAL	AX,1	AX=I1*4
16		SAL	AX,1	AX=I1*8
17		MOV	I1,AX	I1=I1*8
18		LES	DI,[BP+18]	get address of I2
19		MOV	AX,ES:[DI]	AX=I2
20		SAL	AX,1	AX=I2*2
21		SAL	AX,1	AX=I2*4
22		SAL	AX,1	AX=I2*8
23		MOV	I2,AX	I2=I2*8
24		LES	DI,[BP+10]	get address of I3
25		MOV	AX,ES:[DI]	AX=I3
26		SAL	AX,1	AX=I3*2
27		SAL	AX,1	AX=I3*4
28		SAL	AX,1	AX=I3*8
29		MOV	I3,AX	I3=I3*8
30		LES	DI,[BP+34]	get address of S
31		FLD	ES:QWORD PTR[DI]	push S onto FPU stack
32		LDS	SI,[BP+30]	get address of V1
33		LES	DI,[BP+22]	get address of V2
34		MOV	AX,ES	save address of V2 in AX:BX
35		MOV	BX,DI	move destination index into BX
36		LES	DI,[BP+14]	get address of V3
37		MOV	DX,ES	save address of V3 in DX:BP
38		MOV	BP,DI	move destination index into base pointer
39	VPIV1:	FLD	ST(0)	duplicate S on FPU stack
40		FMUL	DS:QWORD PTR[SI]	S*V1
41		ADD	SI,I1	increment address OF V1
42		MOV	ES,AX	move in address of V2
43		MOV	DI,BX	move in address of V2
44		FADD	ES:QWORD PTR[DI]	S*V1+V2
45		ADD	BX,I2	increment address OF V2
46		MOV	ES,DX	move in address of V3
47		MOV	DI,BP	move in address of V3
48		FSTP	ES:QWORD PTR[DI]	pop V3 off FPU stack
49		ADD	BP,I3	increment address OF V3
50		LOOP	VPIV1	loop
51		FPOP		pop S off FPU stack
52	VPIV2:	POP	DS	recover data segment
53		POP	SI	recover source index
54		POP	DI	recover destination index
55		POP	BP	recover base pointer
56		RET	32	return and pop 32 bytes off CPU stack
57	VPIV	ENDP		end of procedure

Note that both the extra segment (ES) and data segment (DS) registers are used, as in this far memory mode addressing there is no guarantee that the arrays will all be in the same segment, something that isn't a concern in most 32-bit and 64-bit codes. Also notice the 3 consecutive shift lefts (SHLs) in steps 14-16, 20-22, and 25-28, which are necessary because the target processor won't accept an immediate SHL AX,3. It would accept a looped shift left (MOV CL,3 followed SHL AX,CL) but this would take longer and also involve the CX register, which we reserve for the main loop. When you exclude the setup and restore steps, the inner loop consists of steps 39-50, which are performed quickly and are almost identical for 32-bit and 64-bit modes, requiring only minor adjustments (viz., DI to EDI to RDI and SI to ESI to RSI).

With inline assembler we don't even need to worry about the first and last sections of the code above, because the C compiler will insert these instructions. Furthermore, we can easily create a FORTRAN callable function in C taking advantage of inline assembler and simply link this at the final stage of creating the executable. In this way, we don't technically need a separate assembler. We will use this method of mixed programming in several of the forthcoming examples. As we shall see, there are even some advantages to writing procedures in FORTRAN 90 so that we can call them from C because someone has already done the hard work of encoding various matrix operations for you.

Chapter 7. Computationally Intensive Functions

Before we delve into more vector instructions, we must first discuss some more basic concepts vital to creating efficient code. The first of these topics will be mathematical functions. FPUs are designed to provide rapid calculation of a few common functions, including: square root, sine, cosine, and tangent. However, there are many more functions that are less common but also vital. We will consider two of these that often arise when solving differential equations: the Gauss error function (erf) and the first exponential integral (E_1).

Error Function

The Gauss error function is defined by the following integral:

$$erf(x) = \frac{2}{\sqrt{\pi}} \int_0^x e^{-t^2} dt \tag{7.1}$$

I have personal history with the error function described elsewhere[6,7,8]. An extremely expensive to remediate (and also detrimental to public health) disaster occurred when someone (before I became involved) used an inaccurate approximation (truncated infinite series) to the error function when designing a contaminant barrier (isolation cap). I noticed the problem immediately and quickly corrected it. After fixing this plus an additional modeling error (over simplification of transport in a granular media), the calculations agreed quite well with the already observed behavior of the contaminant (PCBs) at the site (Housatonic River). When I asked why this (fatal) simplification had been used in the first place, I was told that more terms had been considered but this took far too long to arrive at a result and so was deemed impractical. They could have bought several tractor-trailers full of computers for what this simplification ultimately cost them.

There is more than one way to approach this problem and we will consider two here: infinite series and polynomial approximation. First, the error function can be represented by the following infinite series:

$$erf(x) = \frac{2}{\sqrt{\pi}} \left(x - \frac{x^3}{3} + \frac{x^5}{5 \cdot 2!} - \frac{x^7}{7 \cdot 3!} + ... \right) \tag{7.2}$$

The question then becomes: how many terms are needed to achieve acceptable accuracy? We can easily find out by comparing a limited number of terms to the result when we continue the series until the terms are so small that

---

[6] Benton, D. J., "Modeling Transport of PCBs in a Sorbing and Retarding Medium," USEPA GE-100500-AADY, 1999.
[7] Benton, D. J., "Contaminant Transport In Granular Media: A Case Study In Computational Modeling," *Contaminant Transport*, 2018.
[8] Benton, D. J., "PCBs: A Costly Error" in *Overwhelming Evidence: A Pilgrimage*, ISBN-9798515642211, Amazon, 2021.

they no longer impact the calculation. The code related to this problem may be found in the online archive accompanying this text in folder examples\erf+E1. The archive can be found at the link listed below the Preface. The following table shows the largest error over the domain (-π to +π):

Table 7.1 Infinite Series (erf) Truncation Error

terms	error
4	55.730451860
5	99.991616093
6	151.503599633
7	198.544364056
8	229.197102603
9	236.424852750
10	220.438167697
11	187.524157392
12	146.685178350
13	106.200889688
14	71.568729264
15	45.110893807
16	26.708181290
17	14.908488501
18	7.872053048
19	3.943596591
20	1.879323982
21	0.854001601
22	0.370860559
23	0.154213091
24	0.061515044
25	0.023578590
26	0.008697633
27	0.003092085
28	0.001060826
29	0.000351653
30	0.000112762
31	0.000035015
32	0.000010540
33	0.000003078
34	0.000000873
35	0.000000241
36	0.000000065
37	0.000000017
38	0.000000004
39	0.000000001

Since the range of the error function is (-1 to +1), an error of 151.5 is alarming, but this is what the failed analysis was based on by arbitrarily limiting the calculation to 6 terms. It takes more like 39 or 40 terms to obtain sufficient accuracy. While 40 terms might be a little time consuming it would have been a better decision. There is another way: approximation. The following one comes from the *Handbook of Mathematical Functions*[9] and provides accuracy of $\leq 1.5 \times 10^{-7}$.

$$\text{erf } x = 1 - (a_1 t + a_2 t^2 + a_3 t^3 + a_4 t^4 + a_5 t^5) e^{-x^2} + \epsilon(x)$$

$$t = \frac{1}{1+px}$$

$$|\epsilon(x)| \leq 1.5 \times 10^{-7}$$

$$p = .3275911$$

$$a_1 = .254829592$$
$$a_2 = -.284496736$$
$$a_3 = 1.421413741$$
$$a_4 = -1.453152027$$
$$a_5 = 1.061405429$$

(7.3)

We now consider the computational time (also in testerf.c).

```
testing erf functions
series: 3.9525 seconds
approx: 0.5660 seconds
ratio: 6.98284
```

We have selected a number of terms (40) sufficient to achieve the same accuracy as the approximation. The times above are for 4,000,000 function calls. As we see the approximation is almost seven (6.98) times as fast as the truncated series, which I have found to be typical; that is, it is rarely efficient to use a truncated infinite series for any calculation.

Exponential Integral

The first exponential integral is given by the following expression:

$$E_1(x) = \int_x^\infty \frac{e^{-t}}{t} dt \qquad (7.4)$$

which can be expanded to the following infinite series where γ is Euler's constant 0.577215665:

$$E_1(x) = -\gamma - \ln x - \sum_{k=1}^\infty \frac{(-x)^k}{k \cdot k!} \qquad (7.5)$$

We will now consider $E_1()$ in the same way as erf(). The corresponding code (teste1.c) can be found in the examples\erf+E1 folder. We first calculate how many terms are necessary to achieve convergence over the domain (0.025

---

[9] Abramowitz, M. and I. A. Stegun, *Handbook of Mathematical Functions* first published by the National Bureau of Standards as Technical Monograph No. 55. This invaluable reference may be obtained free online as a PDF from several different web sites.

to 10) using the truncated infinite series in Equation 7.5. The results are shown in this next table.

Table 7.1 Infinite Series (E_1) Truncation Error

terms	error
3	37.612952819
4	66.345536712
5	99.904879746
6	130.883024768
7	151.573110614
8	157.208819261
9	147.608503120
10	126.589919228
11	99.907042042
12	73.024960783
13	49.705597908
14	31.656622212
15	18.943446505
16	10.690207020
17	5.707764855
18	2.891807340
19	1.393924055
20	0.640780496
21	0.281526623
22	0.118447866
23	0.047809961
24	0.018544519
25	0.006922861
26	0.002490839
27	0.000864906
28	0.000290194
29	0.000094189
30	0.000029606
31	0.000009021
32	0.000002667
33	0.000000766
34	0.000000214
35	0.000000058
36	0.000000015
37	0.000000004
38	0.000000001

We see a similar convergence behavior for this function as before. The approximation (also from Abramowitz & Stegun) is:

$$xe^x E_1(x) = \frac{x^2 + a_1 x + a_2}{x^2 + b_1 x + b_2} + \epsilon(x)$$

$1 \leq x < \infty$
$|\epsilon(x)| < 5 \times 10^{-5}$

$a_1 = 2.334733$
$a_2 = .250621$
$b_1 = 3.330657$
$b_2 = 1.681534$

(7.6)

We now consider the computational time (also in teste1.c).

```
testing E1 functions
series: 2.3842 seconds
approx: 0.3156 seconds
ratio: 7.55411
```

which yields a similar result to the previous example for erf(). The approximation is almost eight (7.55) times as fast as the truncated series.

Take-Away

When you are building a model that uses analytical functions such as erf() or E_1() or Bessel functions or the Gamma function or the Beta function, consider using a curve-fit rather than a truncated infinite series. It's worth the effort up front to save computational time later.

Chapter 8. Computationally Intensive Procedures

It is not always obvious what sections of a code consume the most time. I have often found that a single section of the whole may take 99% or even more of the total time. Loops are a good place to start when considering efficiency, especially nested loops, which may not always be apparent. A loop calling a function that contains another loop is an example of this. Before we consider any more vector instructions, we will consider procedures of a more general nature.

Example: Pumped Aquifer Analysis

To illustrate the task of investigating which procedure takes what percentage of the total runtime, we will use a program that I wrote to analyze pumped wells. We don't want to dig up an entire field and even if we did, we couldn't discern it's hydraulic properties before excavation. Instead, we pulse pump one or more wells and measure the response at the pumped well and perhaps one or more surrounding wells. Drilling wells can be quite expensive, so we want to extract the most information from what we have.

The governing equation for a confined aquifer subjected to pumping is attributed to Theis[10,11]. You can find some interesting discussion at the following two websites:

https://transientgroundwaterflow.readthedocs.io/en/latest/TransientFlowToAWell.html

http://www.aqtesolv.com/theis.htm

The analytical solution (discussed in detail in both of the websites listed above) contains the exponential integral we considered in the last chapter so this gives us an opportunity to use that formulation in a practical analysis. The drawdown equation is:

$$d = \left(\frac{Q}{4\pi T}\right) E_1\left(\frac{r^2 S}{4Tt}\right) \tag{8.1}$$

where d is the drawdown [distance], Q is the pumping [volumetric flow rate], T is the transmissivity (similar to conductance in an electrical circuit), r is the radius, S is the storativity (similar to capacitance in an electrical circuit), and t is the time. As we don't know the transmissivity and storativity, this is why we pump the well to find out. Mathematically, we find the values of T and S that best fit the data we collected. We do this through the process of nonlinear minimization, the discussion of which is beyond the scope of this text; however,

---

[10] Charles Vernon Theis (1900-1987) mathematical hydrologist

[11] Theis, C.V., "The Relation between the Lowering of the Piezometric Surface and the Rate and Duration of Discharge of a Well Using Groundwater Storage," Transactions of the American Geophysical Union, Vol. 16, pp. 519-524, 1935.

I refer the reader to my book, *Numerical Methods for Solving Nonlinear Equations*, https://www.amazon.com/dp/B07FL7JR1J

The data and best solution is shown in the following figure:

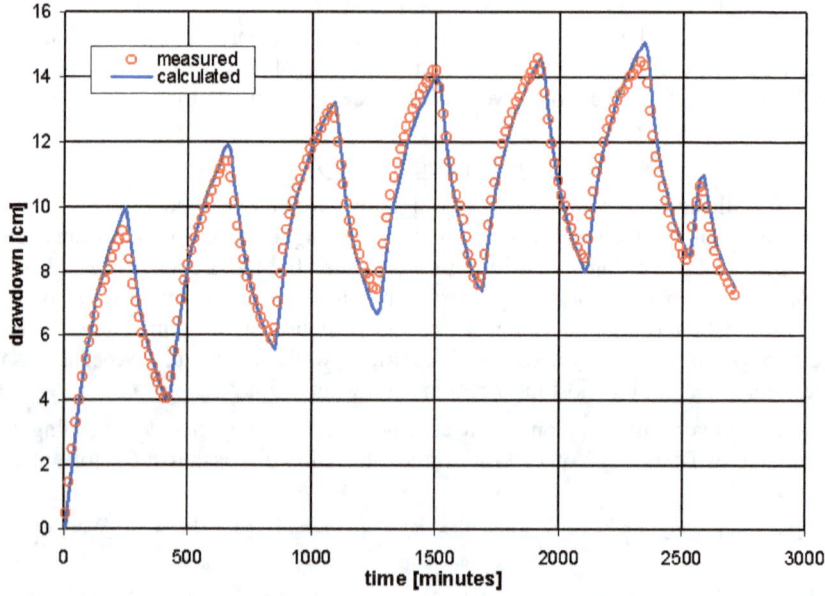

Figure 5. Response of Pumped Aquifer

Finding the best values of T and S is rather involved and there are several ways of approaching this problem. We could search through all possible values with a fine grid but this would be quite computationally intensive. Instead, we use a sophisticated technique called Broyden's method[12]. This approach is described in detail in this SIAM paper[13]. As T and S can vary over a considerable range, it works well to search using the log of these quantities and also display the solution graphically on log scales.

---

[12] Broyden, C., "A New Method of Solving Nonlinear Simultaneous Equations," *Computational Journal*, Vol. 12, pp. 94-99, 1969.

[13] Benton, D. J., "Applications of a Hybrid Derivative-Free Algorithm for Locating Extrema," SIAM SEAS, 1991.

The solution domain is illustrated in this next figure by way of the residual or the sum of the squares of the differences in drawdown between the measured and calculated values:

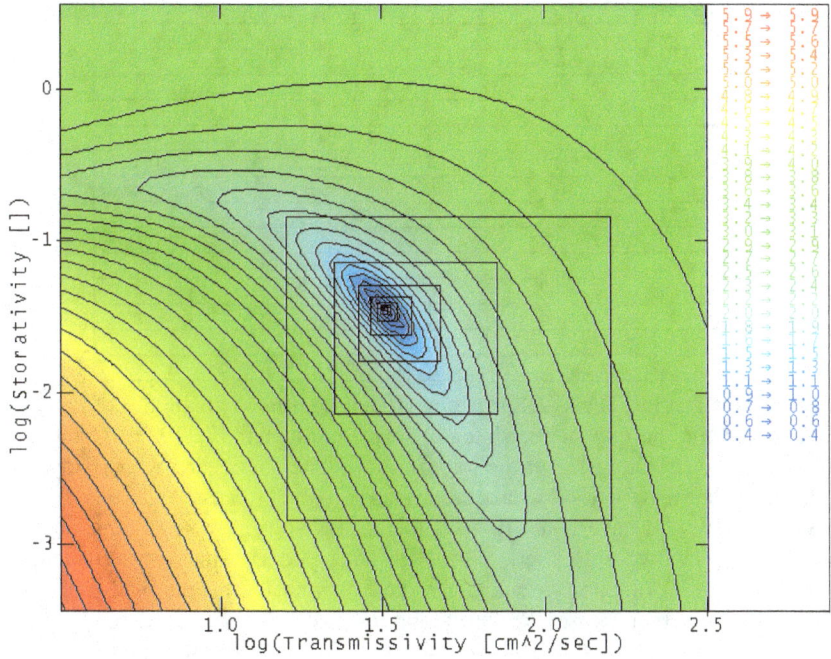

Figure 6. Solution Domain (Residuals)

The solution (optimal values of $T \approx 32$ and $S \approx 0.036$) is inside the blue circle in the middle of the graph. To find this we create a function that returns the residual. That function calls the Theis well function, which calls the first exponential integral function, E_1. The residual function is called many times by the Broyden function, which also calls a matrix solver (Gauss-Jordan elimination) so that the entire process utilizes a variety of procedures. We compile the code as described in Appendix F to determine how many times each procedure is called and how long this takes.

An alternate method for finding the optimum solution is a boxed search in which several values are tested (in this case 3×3), the best is chosen, and the size of the box is reduced by a factor of 2. The solution of sequentially smaller boxes is shown in the preceding figure. There are two batch files provided (_compile.bat and _cOmpile.bat) to compile the program. The first will produce Figure 5 and the second will produce Figure 6.

The function calls and timing are listed in the following table:

Table 8.1 Pumped Aquifer Model Function Timing

num calls	tree ms	function ms	%	per call	func name
66,708	2,206,518	1,802,948	76.4808%	27	Head
888,998	403,569	403,569	17.1193%	0	expi
326	2,332,709	133,315	5.6552%	408	residual
326	2,337,637	4,927	0.2090%	15	Residual
1	763,148	4,390	0.1862%	4,390	Broyden
1	9,656	2,532	0.1074%	2,532	DrawdownGraph
1	2,346,306	1,987	0.0843%	1,987	FindProperties
1,025	1,870	1,870	0.0793%	1	Vdot
1	1,252	1,252	0.0531%	1,252	ReadInput
344	211	211	0.0090%	0	Vcpy
1	2,357,386	170	0.0072%	170	main
450	132	132	0.0056%	0	randbetween
93	74	74	0.0031%	0	Gauss
2	2	2	0.0001%	1	Vset

We see that the Theis well function (Head) consumed 76.4808% of the total runtime, while the exponential integral (expi) consumed 17.1193%. Combined these consumed 93.6002% of the total runtime. The nonlinear solver (Broyden) consumed a mere 0.1862% and the matrix solve (Gauss) consumed only 0.0031%. We did save some time in the matrix solver by separating out the vector copy (Vcpy), fill (Vset), and dot product (Vdot), which is equivalent to Excel's SUMSQ function. Reading the data, writing the results, and preparing the plot files were a miniscule contribution in this case.

In the left column we see that the E_1 function was called almost a million times (888,998), which is why we focused on making this as efficient as possible in the last chapter. This example is dominated by an analytical solution. We next consider an example built around a numerical solution of a different problem. More on this approach and algorithm can be found in several publications[14] plus details on the software can be found on the website listed beneath the Preface.

<u>Example: Buoyant Thermal Plume</u>

The next example we will consider is a buoyant thermal plume discharged into a flowing, thermally-stratified ambient. This particular problem uses 4th order Runge-Kutta to solve the ODE, which is the conservation of mass, linear momentum, and energy. It uses an auxiliary function to calculate the density of

---

[14] Young, S. C., D. J. Benton, J. C. Herweijer, and P. Sims, "The Usefulness of Multi-Well Aquifer Tests in Heterogeneous Aquifers," *International Conference on Transport and Mass Exchange in Sand and Gravel Aquifers*, CRNL, 1990.

water, which is a curve-fit. The model is described in several reports[15,16]. The solution methodology is described in two of my other books[17,18]. The software is also described in more detail along with illustrations on my website listed beneath the Preface. This code (plume2d.c) also includes Broyden's Method and Gauss-Jordan elimination procedures, which are used to find the 6 optimal "tuning" parameters to best-fit field measurements, which are described in the 2002 paper. For the purposes of timing, these features are not used; rather, the final results of the optimization are used once. The model results are shown in this next figure:

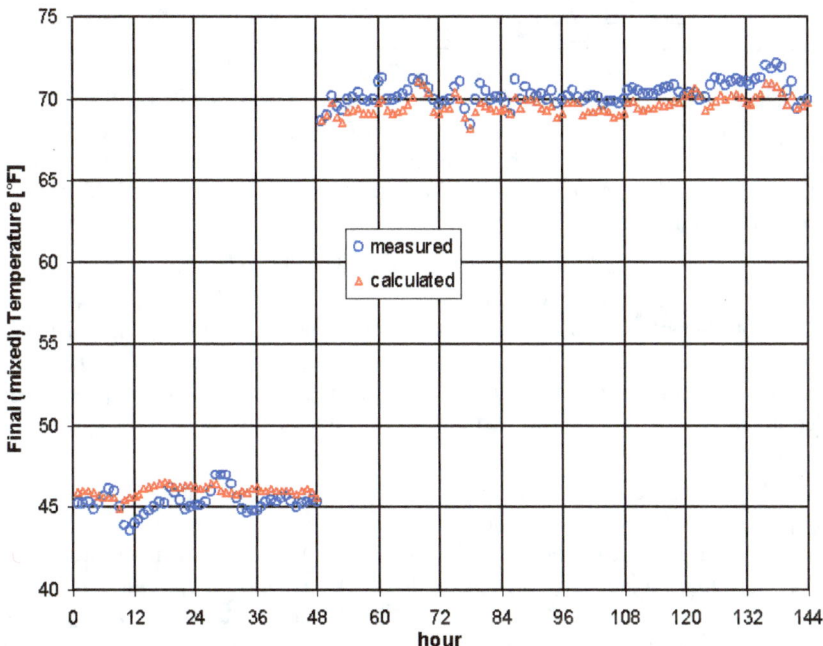

Figure 7. Buoyant Thermal Plume Model Results

---

[15] Benton, D. J., "Development of a Two-Dimensional Plume Model for Positively and Negatively Buoyant Discharges into a Stratified Flowing Ambient," Tennessee Water Resources Association Symposium, 1989.

[16] Benton, D. J., "A Simplified Approach for Modeling a Thermal Plume in a Stratified Ambient," SQNP Report to TVA for the USEPA, February, 2002.

[17] Benton, D. J., *Plumes: Delineation & Transport*, ISBN-9781702292771, Amazon, 2019.

[18] Benton, D. J., *Differential Equations: Numerical Methods for Solving*, ISBN-9781983004162, Amazon, 2018.

The procedure timing is listed in the following table:

Table 8.2 Buoyant Plume Model Function Timing

num calls	tree ms	function ms	%	per call	func name
74,648	321,611	256,173	49.8510%	3	ODE
18,662	421,131	99,519	19.3663%	5	RK4
288	511,528	78,953	15.3642%	274	Plume2D
168,246	50,337	50,337	9.7955%	0	density
74,648	20,883	20,883	4.0638%	0	interpolate
18,950	5,661	5,661	1.1016%	0	fmin
2	513,575	1,440	0.2802%	720	SolveOnce
2	512,135	606	0.1179%	303	Solutions
1	513,877	301	0.0586%	301	main

Here we see that the ODE itself consumed the most (49.85%) with 4th Order Runge-Kutta (RK4) a distant second (19.37%) and the setup (Plume2D) even less (15.36%). The water density function (a curve-fit) consumed only 9.8% of the total time, illustrating the benefit of optimizing this beforehand. The other procedures were negligible.

Example: Saint-Venant/MacCormack Scheme

The next example we will consider is a reservoir model in which we solve the Saint-Venant[19] equation using the MacCormack[20] scheme. This particular problem arises from control of Chickamauga Reservoir. The upstream dam is Watts Bar and the downstream is Chickamauga. The plant in question is Sequoyah Nuclear, located in Soddy Daisy, Tennessee, where I have performed many studies.

The Saint-Venant equation describes a shallow water wave, which propagates back-and-forth between the two dams as a result of starting and stopping the flow at either end. The operation of these dams is controlled to meet multiple objectives, including: hydroelectric power production, flood control, navigation, recreation, and aquatic habitat maintenance. Opening and closing the control gates produces a sloshing effect, which is of particular interest at the nuclear plant, where a large discharge of hot water enters the river. The thermal plume this produces was the subject of the previous example.

---

[19] Adhémar Jean Claude Barré de Saint-Venant (1797-1886) mathematician and fluid mechanician https://en.wikipedia.org/wiki/Shallow_water_equations

[20] MacCormack, R. W., "The Effect of Viscosity in Hypervelocity Impact Cratering," AIAA Paper 69-354, 1969. https://en.wikipedia.org/wiki/MacCormack_method

Typical flows are shown below:

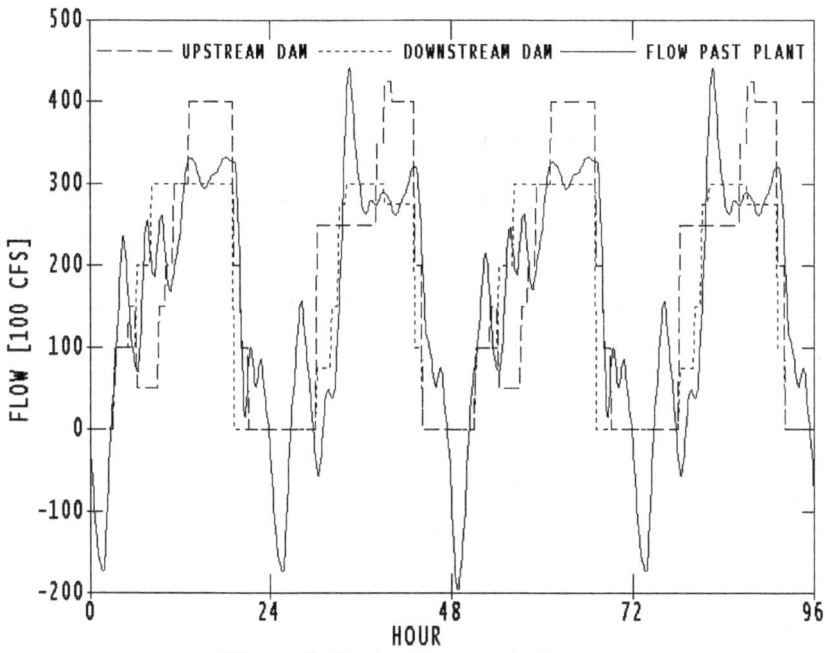

Figure 8. Typical Reservoir Flows

The code (MacCormack.c) includes several procedures, including geometry (cross-sectional area and width vs. depth) and finite difference method (FDM) calculations as well as an outer loop to prepare inputs for the model and process outputs for summary and graphics. Instead of a curve-fit, the geometry calculations utilize look-up tables with linear interpolation. The timings are:

Table 8.3 MacCormack Model Function Timing

num calls	tree ms	function ms	%	per call	func name
4	186,625	169,369	89.9722%	42,342	Routing
2,880	12,361	12,361	6.5664%	4	MacCormack
50,400	2,456	2,456	1.3047%	0	fmax
50,400	2,433	2,433	1.2925%	0	fmin
1	188,246	1,621	0.8611%	1,621	main
1	4	4	0.0021%	4	Geometry

Here we see that the FDM calculations (Routing) took most of the time (~90%) with the setup (MacCormack) at a distant second (6.6%). The geometry calculations consumed a mere 0.0021%, illustrating how fast a look-up table can be compared to even a simple polynomial curve-fit. This particular reservoir model does not lend itself to vector processing but was one of the models run on the CDC mainframe back in the day.

Example: Kinematic Wave Equation

Our last example in this chapter is a different type of reservoir model. This time we consider a stream (the Clinch River), which can at various times run dry. The previous Saint-Venant equation only applies to a channel that never dries out. Temperature was a particular concern with this application, as the cooling water for Bull Run Steam Plant is drawn from the Clinch. It's also a personal interest, having spent much time there plus I can see the stack from my home plus a friend (Chuck Bowman) did the thermal design[21]. For this stream we use the kinematic wave equation[22,23]. Model results are shown in this next figure:

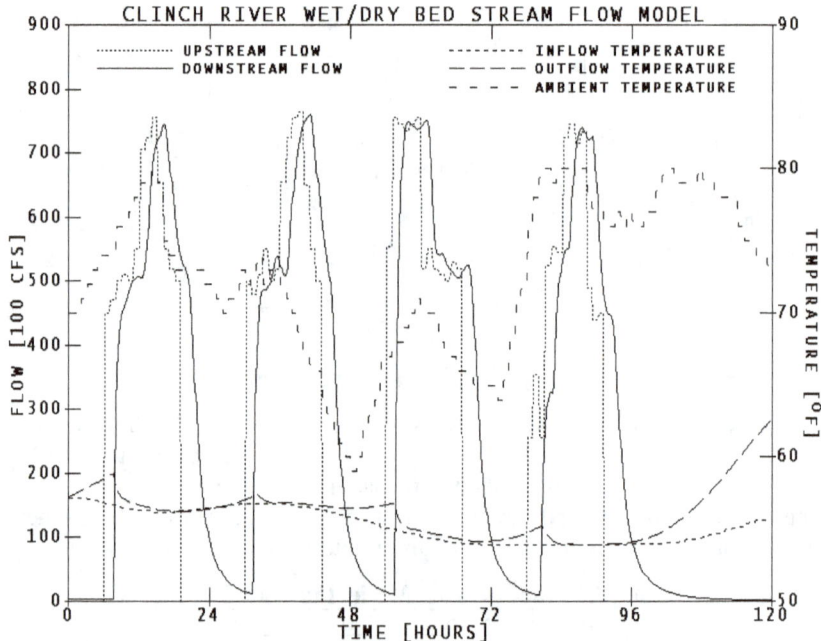

Figure 9. Kinematic Wave Model Results

---

[21] Bowman, C. F. and S. N. Bowman, *Thermal Engineering of Nuclear Power Stations: Balance-of-Plant Systems*, CRC Press, 2020.
[22] https://www.hec.usace.army.mil/confluence/hmsdocs/hmstrm/surface-runoff/kinematic-wave-model
[23] more details on kinematic wave models https://pubs.usgs.gov/pp/1302/report.pdf

The procedure timing is listed in the following table:

Table 8.4 Kinematic Wave Model Function Timing

num calls	tree ms	function ms	% ms	per call	func name
1,200	5,874,414	2,781,200	47.2430%	2,317	Routing
1,396	1,459,546	1,283,263	21.7982%	919	DryBed
175,639	850,921	754,274	12.8125%	4	Corrector
1,447,682	395,816	395,816	6.7236%	0	fmax
939,360	250,566	250,566	4.2563%	0	fmin
3,377	243,687	216,856	3.6836%	64	Advance
3,377	217,909	191,691	3.2562%	56	Predictor
1	5,887,006	12,592	0.2139%	12,592	main
1,396	743	743	0.0126%	0	FlipFlop
1	1	1	0.0000%	1	Geometry

This model uses a predictor/corrector approach. We see that the routing model itself (which includes setup, iterations, and calling the supporting procedures) consumes almost half (47.2%) of the runtime. The dry bed (heat transfer calculations) takes a little more than one-fifth (21.8%) of the time, which is not surprising. The corrector step (12.8%) takes 4× as long as the predictor step (3.3%). As with the last example, the geometry calculations (which use a look-up table) take a negligible fraction of the time (<0.0000%). This model also does not lend itself to vector processing but was one of the reservoir models run on the CDC mainframe back in the day.

Chapter 9. Basic Matrix Operations

We next consider basic matrix operations. These can be performed automatically by a FORTRAN 90 compiler, such as my personal favorite: Compaq Visual Fortran Optimizing Compiler Version 6.1 Sadly, this wonderful tool is no longer available following the demise of Compaq. If you can't afford the Intel™ FORTRAN compiler the next best thing might be Watcom, which is available on GitHub and SourceForge. If you're really desperate, there's always GNU as a last resort.

F90 provides a convenient way of comparing ordinary loop instructions to optimized ones. By activating the /Fa option, you can see the instructions created by the compiler so as to compare the two. Consider the most basic operation: matrix copy. Below we have the FORTRAN 77 and 90 versions:

```
SUBROUTINE COPYF77(A,B,M,N)
IMPLICIT INTEGER*4(I-N),REAL*8(A-H,O-Z)
DIMENSION A(M,N),B(M,N)
DO I=1,M
  DO J=1,N
    B(I,J)=A(I,J)
  ENDDO
ENDDO
RETURN
END
SUBROUTINE COPYF90(A,B,M,N)
IMPLICIT INTEGER*4(I-N),REAL*8(A-H,O-Z)
DIMENSION A(M,N),B(M,N)
B=A
RETURN
END
```

The following code copies a 1000×1000 double-precision (REAL*8) matrix copied 500 times using each method (F77 and F90):

```
PARAMETER (M=1000,N=1000)
SUBROUTINE TESTCOPY(A,B,M,N)
IMPLICIT INTEGER*4(I-N),REAL*8(A-H,O-Z)
REAL*8 A(M,N),B(M,N)
CALL CPU_TIME(T1)
DO K=1,500
   CALL COPYF77(A,B,M,N)
ENDDO
CALL CPU_TIME(T2)
DO K=1,500
   CALL COPYF90(A,B,M,N)
ENDDO
CALL CPU_TIME(T3)
WRITE(*,'(A)')'MATRIX COPY'
WRITE(*,'(A,F6.3)')'F77=',T2-T1
```

```
          WRITE(*,'(A,F6.3)')'F90=',T3-T2
          WRITE(*,'(A,F5.1)')'RATIO=',(T2-T1)/(T3-T2);
          RETURN
          END
```
and the results are:
```
     MATRIX COPY
     F77= 2.656
     F90= 0.125
     RATIO= 21.3
```

We see from this example that optimized instructions using the same hardware are 21× faster than non-optimized ones. For this operation the core instructions are the same:
```
     FLD   QWORD PTR[EBP]
     SUB   EBX,4
     LEA   EBP,DWORD PTR[EBP]
     FSTP  QWORD PTR[EAX]
     LEA   EAX,DWORD PTR[EAX]
     CMP   EBX,3
```

The difference in this case is how the loops are handled. Of course, if we are simply copying values from one matrix to another, we can do much better than this by using the CPU instructions and not involving the FPU at all:
```
    1 MOV ECX,m
    2 MUL ECX,n
    3 SHL ECX,1
    4 LEA ESI[a]
    5 LEA EDI[b]
    6 REP MOVSD
```

Step 1 loads m into the loop register (ECX). Step 2 multiplies this by n. Step 3 multiplies this by 1 (shift left), which accounts for REAL*8s being twice the size of int32s. Steps 4 and 5 load the source and destination indices (ESI and EDI) and step 6 does the rest (DWORD copy, not a literal *move*, repeated ECX times). We next consider matrix addition. The F77 and F90 codes are:
```
          SUBROUTINE ADDF77(A,B,C,M,N)
          IMPLICIT INTEGER*4(I-N),REAL*8(A-H,O-Z)
          DIMENSION A(M,N),B(M,N),C(M,N)
          DO I=1,M
            DO J=1,N
              C(I,J)=A(I,J)+B(I,J)
            ENDDO
          ENDDO
          RETURN
          END
          SUBROUTINE ADDF90(A,B,C,M,N)
          IMPLICIT INTEGER*4(I-N),REAL*8(A-H,O-Z)
          DIMENSION A(M,N),B(M,N),C(M,N)
```

```
       C=A+B
       RETURN
       END
```
and the results are:
```
MATRIX ADD
F77= 3.578
F90= 0.141
RATIO= 25.4
```

Again, we see a significant advantage (25×) with the optimized instructions. Of course, in this case (adding floating-point values) we must use the FPU. We next consider nine matrix operations (copy, transpose, scalar addition, scalar multiplication, scalar division, matrix addition, matrix subtraction, inversion, and solution) in a single code (speed*.* in folder examples\F90). We use Gauss-Jordan elimination with full row and column pivoting for the inversion and solution process.

The code is divided into 5 files: speed.c (the main program that calls all the others), speeduc.c (unoptimized C), speedoc.c (optimized C), speed77.for (FORTRAN 77), and speed90.for (FORTRAN 90). Compiling and linking these files depends on which compilers you are using. They are currently arranged for the Zortec, Symantec, or Digital Mars C compiler and the Compaq FORTRAN compiler. The former creates and expects object modules in the OMF[24] format, while the latter creates object modules in the COFF[25] format so that the converter (COFF2OMF) is required before linking. Minor modifications may be required when using VS FORTRAN or the Intel™ compilers or GNU.

Table 9.1 Comparison of Operation Times

operation	unopt C	opti C	FTN77	FTN90	slow/fast
scalar add	0.051876	0.022777	0.116524	0.014122	8.3
scalar multiply	0.052851	0.021939	0.116562	0.014326	8.1
scalar divide	0.219729	0.207336	0.216828	0.219529	1.1
matrix copy	0.049976	0.014941	0.116847	0.013879	8.4
matrix transpose	0.049317	0.039823	0.041392	0.046516	4.3
matrix addition	0.073353	0.029886	0.155081	0.020788	7.5
matrix subtract	0.073988	0.030277	0.164352	0.021440	7.7
matrix inversion	0.332131	0.388233	0.192964	0.183522	2.1
matrix solution	0.243575	0.061671	0.090419	0.084311	3.9

Note that some of the tasks in the preceding table are repeated several times to consume sufficient time for comparison. The first 7 are performed 200 times and the last 2 are performed only once. The matrices are double-precision and have dimension 359×359=128,881 elements. This particular size was selected to avoid a "quirk" in the F90 transpose operation for this particular compiler. The other F90 operations could be much larger without issue.

---

[24] Object Module Format (OMF) used by some early (e.g., Intel 386) 32-bit compilers
[25] Common Object File Format (COFF) object-code format for UNIX and also Microsoft

Scalar Add and Multiply

We see in this table for the scalar add that optimized C (well-crafted loops) is about 2× faster than non-optimized C (the usual loops). Non-optimized C is almost 2× faster than F77 (conventional FORTRAN). The real surprise is that F90 is almost 2× faster than optimized C. This is where the stories come from that FORTRAN is faster than C for big models. While there is some basis for these claims, as we shall see, it is not always the case and the real situation is more complicated than that. It does mean that you might want to take advantage of such features by calling F90 procedures from some other code. Let us consider the two subroutines:

```
SUBROUTINE SCALARADD77(A,B,C,M,N)
IMPLICIT INTEGER*4(I-N),REAL*8(A-H,O-Z)
DIMENSION A(M,N),C(N,M)
DO I=1,M
  DO J=1,N
    C(I,J)=A(I,J)+B
  ENDDO
ENDDO
RETURN
END
SUBROUTINE SCALARADD90(A,B,C,M,N)
IMPLICIT INTEGER*4(I-N),REAL*8(A-H,O-Z)
DIMENSION A(M,N),C(N,M)
C=A+B
RETURN
END
```

There are no loops in the F90 code because the compiler knows what to do. If you want to compare the respective instructions, these can be found in SPEED77.asm and SPEED90.asm located in the examples\F90 folder of the online archive. In all 4 encodings the FPU is used for the core operation so that the difference in speeds are entirely due to the surrounding code, setting up and executing the loop(s) and cleaning up afterward.

We see almost the same numbers for the scalar multiply because the FADD and FMUL instructions take a similar number of ticks to accomplish and most of the cost here is the surrounding code. The respective FORTRAN codes are identical except for *B instead of +B.

Scalar Divide

We see a completely different behavior for the scalar divide. All 4 encodings are essentially the same speed. Why? Because the FDIV instruction takes a lot longer than the FADD and FMUL. While the supporting code is important in the scalar add and multiply, it's not as significant a contribution to runtime in the scalar divide. This is why you will read some articles online that say FORTRAN is so much faster, while there are just as many that claim this is not true. They may both be telling the truth depending on what tests or examples or model(s) they were comparing. If you hope to really get the most out of your hardware, you will have to work harder than that.

Matrix Copy

We next consider the matrix copy. Here we see that optimized C and F90 take about the same time as does non-optimized C and F77 with the former being about 8× faster than the latter. This shouldn't be surprising, as we have shown before, we can do even better than this with REP MOVSD or REP MOVSQ.

Matrix Transpose

The matrix transpose is next. This operation flips a matrix (which is not necessarily square) about the diagonal. I must insert here that I have more than once seen code that implemented a matrix transpose the lazy way: copying the elements to another matrix and then back into the original. This is bad for two reasons: 1) it requires twice the storage and 2) it requires three times the operations. We always perform an *in-place* matrix transpose, whether in C or FORTRAN, optimized or not. There is a "quirk" in the Compaq compiler that croaks for n>359. Hopefully, this is not present in other F90 compilers. In the table we see that it takes about the same time to perform this operation regardless of the encoding.

Matrix Addition and Subtraction

Next we consider matrix addition and subtraction. As we might expect, these two operations require essentially the same time (add or subtract) and only vary from one encoding to another. This is because the FADD and FSUB instructions take the same time. The non-optimized C is again about 2× faster than F77 and the optimized C is about the same as F90, both of which are about 8× faster than the non-optimized code.

Matrix Inversion and Solution

The final two operations we consider in this chapter are matrix inversion and solution. Both are accomplished using Gauss-Jordan elimination with full row and column pivoting. You must use row pivoting, as some non-singular matrices will appear singular if you don't. Column pivoting is optional but enough examples have been published to more than warrant its use for accuracy, if not avoiding singularities.

We see that inversion takes somewhat longer than solution, which is not surprising, as the latter is most of the former and the same basic procedure is used. FORTRAN is a little faster than C but optimized vs. non-optimized and F90 vs. F77 isn't that much different. This is because most of the work is done by the FPU and not shuffling numbers and indices about. None of these algorithms use the VPIV or any other vector instructions, which we will consider in Chapter 11. This also fuels the fire of arguments over whether FORTRAN is faster than C or not. We do see in the table that F77 and F90 are both faster than either non-optimized or optimized C. As it turns out (at least for this compiler, as can be deduced from comparing the respective assembler encodings) that the FORTRAN compiler does a better job of managing the FPU stack.

With the matrix solution we see that the non-optimized C requires more than 2× the time as F77, while optimized C is only slightly faster than F90. Again, we see that the F77 encoding is almost as fast as the F90. This too is arises from the fact that the process makes particularly intensive use of the FPU.

Chapter 10. Advanced Matrix Operations

While there are several types of advanced matrix operations we might consider, the one we will focus on here is the Singular Value Decomposition (SVD). Experience has shown that other similar complex operations exhibit the same behavior. We will consider specialized matrices and vector solutions in Chapter 11. The SVD recognizes that any matrix, square or rectangular full rank or not and positive definite or not, can be represented by:

$$M = U\Sigma V^T \qquad (10.1)$$

where M is the matrix, U contains the left eigenvectors, Σ contains the singular values, and V contains the right eigenvectors. The eigenvectors are ortho-normal (orthogonal and normal); that is, when multiplied by the transpose yields the identity matrix. Every vector is perpendicular to every other vector and each has a magnitude of unity. For a positive-definite symmetric matrix $U=V$. The matrix Σ is diagonal (all off-diagonal terms are zero). There are a variety of uses for the SVD, one of the most interesting being compressing images such as the ones sent back to Earth by deep space probes.

There are several ways to obtain the SVD. We shall consider two: Householder[26] reflections and the von Mises[27] method or power iteration with deflation. Articles on both of these methods can readily be found on the Web, for example at Wikipedia. The codes (svdtest.c, SVD77.FOR, and SVD90.FOR) can be found in the folder examples\SVD in the online archive. We will only consider optimized C, F77, and F90 for this example. We need a matrix to solve and for the purposes of illustration will use a Vandermonde[28]. This is the matrix you get when curve fitting $p(x)=c_0+c_1x+c_2x^2+c_3x^3+...$ and in particular when $x_1=1, x_2=2, x_3=3,...$ The elements of the matrix can be expressed:

$$V_{ij} = x_i^j \qquad (10.2)$$

---

[26] Alston Scott Householder (1904–1993) American mathematician and biologist
[27] Richard von Mises and H. Pollaczek-Geiringer, "Praktische Verfahren der Gleichungsauflösung (Practical Methods for Solving Equations)," ZAMM - Zeitschrift für Angewandte Mathematik und Mechanik (Journal of Applied Mathematics and Mechanics), Vol. 9, pp. 152-164, 1929.
[28] Alexandre-Théophile Vandermonde (1735–1796) French mathematician, musician, and chemist

We will first compare the two methods (Householder and von Mises) to see how these stack up regardless of how we might encode them. A comparison of runtimes is listed in the table below:

Table 10.1 Comparison of Runtimes

matrix size	seconds Householder	von Mises	ratio P/H
3x3	0.000299	0.000011	0.04
4x4	0.000010	0.000101	10
5x5	0.000013	0.000483	37
6x6	0.000015	0.000883	59
7x7	0.000020	0.001758	88
8x8	0.000023	0.002285	99
9x9	0.000028	0.002945	105
10x10	0.000032	0.003987	125
11x11	0.000038	0.005393	142
12x12	0.000042	0.006286	150
13x13	0.000055	0.008709	158
14x14	0.000059	0.010150	172
15x15	0.000061	0.011756	193
16x16	0.000065	0.013404	206
17x17	0.000084	0.016052	191
18x18	0.000080	0.018881	236
19x19	0.000091	0.023726	261
20x20	0.000099	0.025671	259
25x25	0.000158	0.047661	302
30x30	0.000250	0.085078	340
35x35	0.000363	0.121093	334
40x40	0.000479	0.172353	360
45x45	0.000658	0.235784	358
50x50	0.000900	0.315191	350
55x55	0.001131	0.422608	374
60x60	0.001428	0.522025	366

We see from the right column that the only case where the Householder method isn't much faster than the von Mises is for n<4, which wouldn't matter anyway. If we care about speed, we will always use the Householder method. We next consider the C vs. F77 vs. F90 implementation. As before, the assembler instructions created by the F77 and F90 compilers can be found in SVC77.asm and SVD90.asm, respectively. The Householder algorithm is the same in C, F77, and F90, only the machine-level implementation differs, which is what we're considering here. There are some differences in the F77 and F90 codes, for example a section of the F77:

```
          DO 250 I=1,N
          L=I+1
          TEMP(I)=SCALE*G
          G=0.D0
          S=0.D0
          SCALE=0.D0
          IF(I.GT.M) GO TO 170
```

```
      DO 110 K=I,M
      UKI=U(K,I)
  110 SCALE=SCALE+DABS(UKI)
      IF(SCALE.EQ.0.D0) GO TO 170
      DO 120 K=I,M
      U(K,I)=U(K,I)/SCALE
  120 S=S+U(K,I)**2
      F=U(I,I)
      G=-DSIGN(DSQRT(S),F)
      H=F*G-S
      U(I,I)=F-G
      IF(I.EQ.N) GO TO 150
      DO 140 J=L,N
      S=0.D0
      DO 130 K=I,M
  130 S=S+U(K,I)*U(K,J)
      F=S/H
      DO 140 K=I,M
  140 U(K,J)=U(K,J)+F*U(K,I)
  150 DO 160 K=I,M
  160 U(K,I)=SCALE*U(K,I)
  170 SIGMA(I)=SCALE*G
      G=0.D0
      S=0.D0
      SCALE=0.D0
      IF(I.GT.M.OR.I.EQ.N) GO TO 250
      DO 180 K=L,N
      UIK=U(I,K)
  180 SCALE=SCALE+DABS(UIK)
      IF(SCALE.EQ.0.D0) GO TO 250
      DO 190 K=L,N
      U(I,K)=U(I,K)/SCALE
  190 S=S+U(I,K)**2
      F=U(I,L)
      G=-DSIGN(DSQRT(S),F)
      H=F*G-S
      U(I,L)=F-G
      DO 200 K=L,N
  200 TEMP(K)=U(I,K)/H
      IF(I.EQ.M) GO TO 230
      DO 220 J=L,M
      S=0.D0
      DO 210 K=L,M
  210 S=S+U(J,K)*U(I,K)
      DO 220 K=L,N
  220 U(J,K)=U(J,K)+S*TEMP(K)
  230 DO 240 K=L,N
  240 U(I,K)=SCALE*U(I,K)
  250 ANORM=DMAX1(ANORM,DABS(SIGMA(I))+DABS(TEMP(I)))
```

and the same section in F90:

```
          DO I=1,N
            L=I+1
            TEMP(I)=SCALE*G
            G=0D0
            S=0D0
            SCALE=0D0
            IF(I.LE.M)THEN
              DO K=I,M
                UKI=U(K,I)
                SCALE=SCALE+DABS(UKI)
              ENDDO
              IF(SCALE.NE.0D0)THEN
                DO K=I,M
                  U(K,I)=U(K,I)/SCALE
                  S=S+U(K,I)**2
                ENDDO
                F=U(I,I)
                G=-DSIGN(DSQRT(S),F)
                H=F*G-S
                U(I,I)=F-G
                IF(I.NE.N)THEN
                  DO J=L,N
                  S=0D0
                  DO K=I,M
                  S=S+U(K,I)*U(K,J)
                  ENDDO
                  F=S/H
                  DO K=I,M
                  U(K,J)=U(K,J)+F*U(K,I)
                  ENDDO
                  ENDDO
                ENDIF
                DO K=I,M
                  U(K,I)=SCALE*U(K,I)
                ENDDO
              ENDIF
            ENDIF
            SIGMA(I)=SCALE*G
            G=0D0
            S=0D0
            SCALE=0D0
            IF(.NOT.(I.GT.M.OR.I.EQ.N))THEN
              DO K=L,N
                UIK=U(I,K)
                SCALE=SCALE+DABS(UIK)
              ENDDO
              IF(SCALE.NE.0D0)THEN
                DO K=L,N
```

```
            U(I,K)=U(I,K)/SCALE
            S=S+U(I,K)**2
         ENDDO
         F=U(I,L)
         G=-DSIGN(DSQRT(S),F)
         H=F*G-S
         U(I,L)=F-G
         DO K=L,N
            TEMP(K)=U(I,K)/H
         ENDDO
         IF(I.NE.M)THEN
            DO J=L,M
               S=0D0
               DO K=L,M
                  S=S+U(J,K)*U(I,K)
               ENDDO
               DO K=L,N
                  U(J,K)=U(J,K)+S*TEMP(K)
               ENDDO
            ENDDO
         ENDIF
         DO K=L,N
            U(I,K)=SCALE*U(I,K)
         ENDDO
      ENDIF
   ENDIF
   ANORM=DMAX1(ANORM,DABS(SIGMA(I))+DABS(TEMP(I)))
ENDDO
```

There is some difference in the loops and if...then...else sections but the question is: Does it matter? That is, do things like this make a big enough difference to impact the runtime or not? Just how much can an optimizing compiler do? Can an optimizing compiler clean up sloppy code? The answer is: Maybe, maybe not, perhaps some. Experience has shown that choosing an efficient algorithm is vital to minimizing runtime, as this example (von Mises vs. Householder) illustrates so well (note the 366× speed difference at the bottom of Table 10.1).

Four implementations are compared in this next table:

Table 10.2 Comparison of 4 Implementations

```
         testing singular value decomposition
matrix  vonMises  <-------Householder------>
  size    opt C     opt C      F77         F90
  3x3   0.000017  0.000008  0.000014  0.000012  seconds
  4x4   0.000050  0.000013  0.000013  0.000013  seconds
  5x5   0.001194  0.000025  0.000021  0.000022  seconds
  6x6   0.003036  0.000034  0.000026  0.000027  seconds
  7x7   0.004023  0.000035  0.000038  0.000038  seconds
  8x8   0.005874  0.000046  0.000053  0.000053  seconds
  9x9   0.010552  0.000062  0.000069  0.000069  seconds
 10x10  0.012201  0.000072  0.000082  0.000089  seconds
 15x15  0.038766  0.000154  0.000150  0.000148  seconds
 20x20  0.089779  0.000266  0.000241  0.000234  seconds
 25x25  0.173694  0.000442  0.000383  0.000383  seconds
 30x30  0.290095  0.000653  0.000554  0.000548  seconds
 35x35  0.443320  0.001052  0.000866  0.000856  seconds
 40x40  0.671706  0.001487  0.001186  0.001263  seconds
 45x45  0.923578  0.001889  0.001712  0.001614  seconds
 50x50  1.262706  0.002896  0.002296  0.002362  seconds
 55x55  1.663556  0.003434  0.002717  0.002749  seconds
 60x60  2.164367  0.004470  0.003614  0.003678  seconds
```

In this table we see that there is essentially no difference between the F77 and F90 implementation, indicating that the difference in loops is negligible. The F77 and F90 are both slightly faster than optimized C, again reinforcing the stories that FORTRAN may be faster than C in some cases. Again, the von Mises algorithm is far less attractive than the Householder.

Chapter 11. Banded Matrix Solutions

We next consider a special type of matrix for which there are several solution algorithms, one of which readily lends itself to vectorization. This matrix arises when solving Laplace's Equation[29], which is the governing partial differential equation for heat conduction and diffusion as well as other problems.

$$\frac{\partial^2 T}{\partial x^2} + \frac{\partial^2 T}{\partial y^2} = 0 \qquad (11.1)$$

For simplicity, we apply Dirichlet[30] boundary conditions (i.e., constants) along the sides. The final solution is shown in the following figure:

Figure 10. Solution to Laplace's Equation

---

[29] Pierre-Simon marquis de Laplace (1749–1827) French mathematician, physicist, astronomer, and philosopher
[30] Johann Peter Gustav Lejeune Dirichlet (1805–1859) German mathematician

We will consider three methods for solving this problem: 1) Gauss-Seidel[31] (a.k.a. the Liebmann[32] Method), 2) Successive Over-Relaxation (SOR), and 3) Hestenes-Stiefel (a.k.a. the Conjugate-Gradient Method)[33]. Gauss-Seidel is basically a successive substitution, separating the off-diagonal elements from the diagonal ones. SOR is a modification of Gauss-Seidel with an exaggeration factor (typically 1.5), which often converges faster. The Conjugate-Gradient method is a repeated vector projection with each successive vector approximation to the solution mutually perpendicular to the preceding ones so that theoretically, the final solution must be found in N steps, where N is the rank of the matrix. In practice, an adequate approximation to the solution is often found in far fewer than N steps, making this an attractive approach.

This particular mathematical problem is one of the first I ever attempted to solve using vector instructions. The original code (TBAND.FOR, VIS4.ASM, and VIS8.ASM) still works with only minor modifications and can be found in the online archive in folder examples\tband\F77 and will serve to begin our discussion of this topic. This particular compilation is limited to an 80×80 two-dimensional field of nodes or a total of 6400 equations and unknowns. The output is listed below:

```
TBAND/V2.0: Test Banded matrix solvers
solving the Laplace Equation with
Dirichlet boundary conditions
number of grid points=80*80=6400
solving using Gauss-Seidel
error reduction   .00050  CPU=1.102 sec
solving using Successive Over Relaxation
error reduction   .00050  CPU= .547 sec
solving using vectorized Hestenes-Stiefel
error reduction   .00047  CPU= .172 sec
```

Here we see that SOR is twice as fast as G-S, H-S/C-J is 3.2 times as fast as SOR and 6.4 times as fast as G-S. While this won't be true for every example with these three methods, it does indicate that these approaches are worth considering. All three methods were able to reduce the residual to 0.0005 of the initial estimate, which is adequate for this problem. There are two rather significant limitations for this implementation: 1) it uses single-precision (32-bit) floating-point numbers and 2) the assembler only works in 16-bit mode.

---

[31] Philipp Ludwig von Seidel (1821-1896) German mathematician

[32] Liebmann, H., "Die Angenaherte Ermittlung Harmonischer Funktionen und Konformer Abbildungen (The Approximate Determination of Harmonic Functions and Conformal Maps)," Sitzungsber, Münchener, Vol. 47, pp. 385-416, 1918

[33] Hestenes, M. R. and E. Stiefel, "Methods of Conjugate Gradients for Solving Linear Systems," Journal of Research National Bureau of Standards, Vol. 49, No. 6, pp. 409–436, 1952.

The next step we will consider is migrating the code to 32-bit/64-bit and F90. The assembler portion (i.e., the vector instructions) must also be rewritten but first, we see what happens if the vector instructions are implemented in common F90 rather than assembler. That version of the same code can be found in the folder examples\tband\F90. This implementation can handle much larger matrices and so we expand the 80×80 to 400×400 or 160,000 equations and unknowns.

```
TBAND/V3.0: Test Banded matrix solvers
solving the Laplace Equation with
Dirichlet boundary conditions
number of grid points=400*400=160000
solving using Gauss-Seidel
error reduction 0.0000200   CPU=64.234 sec
solving using Successive Over Relaxation
error reduction 0.0000200   CPU=32.562 sec
solving using vectorized Hestenes-Stiefel
error reduction 0.0000194   CPU= 6.922 sec
```

This implementation is not vectorized (although it could be if we modified the VIS accordingly). We see that SOR is approximately 2×faster then G-S and H-S/C-J is approximately 10×faster, even without the VIS. We will further explore this problem by converting the code from F90 to C, which can be found in the examples\tband\C folder. The results are:

```
TBAND/V3.0: Test Banded matrix solvers
solving the Laplace Equation with
Dirichlet boundary conditions
number of grid points=400*400=160000
creating banded matrix
solving using Gauss-Seidel
error=0, reduction=1.99992E-005, CPU=65.928687 seconds
solving using Successive Over Relaxation
error=0, reduction=1.99989E-005, CPU=33.443553 seconds
solving using vectorized Hestenes-Stiefel
error=0, reduction=1.93974E-005, CPU=6.790828 seconds
saving solution: tband.tb2
```

which is essentially the same as the F90 implementation. For this example we will implement the vector instructions using inline assembler within the C code. There is a variable at the top of the code:

```
#define vectorize 1
```

which can be set to 0 or 1 for conditional compilation. You can set the variable and recompile to change the option. The compiler will also create an assembler listing (tband.asm). First, we will see what happens, then we will discuss why.

The vectorized results are listed below:

```
TBAND/V3.0: Test Banded matrix solvers
solving the Laplace Equation with
Dirichlet boundary conditions
number of grid points=400*400=160000
creating banded matrix
solving using Gauss-Seidel
error=0, reduction=1.99992E-005, CPU=65.625440 seconds
solving using Successive Over Relaxation
error=0, reduction=1.99989E-005, CPU=33.333616 seconds
solving using vectorized Hestenes-Stiefel
error=0, reduction=1.93974E-005, CPU=7.439170 seconds
saving solution: tband.tb2
```

The vectorized results (7.44 sec) is a little slower than the non-vectorized (6.79 sec). Before discussing why, let's look at the inline assembler.

```
void vadd(double*v1,double*v2,double*v3,int n) /* vector
    addition */
{
#if(!vectorize)
   int i;
   for(i=0;i<n;i++)
      v3[i]=v1[i]+v2[i];
#else
   __asm
     {
     push ebx
     push ecx
     push esi
     push edi
     mov  ebx,dword ptr v1
     mov  esi,dword ptr v2
     mov  edi,dword ptr v3
     mov  ecx,n
  l1:fld  qword ptr[ebx]
     fadd qword ptr[esi]
     fstp qword ptr[edi]
     add  ebx,8
     add  esi,8
     add  edi,8
     loop l1
     pop  edi
     pop  esi
     pop  ecx
     pop  ebx
     }
#endif
}
```

```c
void vsub(double*v1,double*v2,double*v3,int n)  /* vector
    subtraction */
{
#if(!vectorize)
  int i;
  for(i=0;i<n;i++)
    v3[i]=v1[i]-v2[i];
#else
  __asm
  {
    push ebx
    push ecx
    push esi
    push edi
    mov  ebx,dword ptr v1
    mov  esi,dword ptr v2
    mov  edi,dword ptr v3
    mov  ecx,n
l1: fld  qword ptr[ebx]
    fsub qword ptr[esi]
    fstp qword ptr[edi]
    add  ebx,8
    add  esi,8
    add  edi,8
    loop l1
    pop  edi
    pop  esi
    pop  ecx
    pop  ebx
  }
#endif
}
void vmpy(double*v1,double*v2,double*v3,int n)  /* vector
    multiply */
{
#if(!vectorize)
  int i;
  for(i=0;i<n;i++)
    v3[i]=v1[i]*v2[i];
#else
  __asm
  {
    push ebx
    push ecx
    push esi
    push edi
    mov  ebx,dword ptr v1
    mov  esi,dword ptr v2
```

```
        mov   edi,dword ptr v3
        mov   ecx,n
   l1:  fld   qword ptr[ebx]
        fmul  qword ptr[esi]
        fstp  qword ptr[edi]
        add   ebx,8
        add   esi,8
        add   edi,8
        loop  l1
        pop   edi
        pop   esi
        pop   ecx
        pop   ebx
        }
#endif
   }

void vdiv(double*v1,double*v2,double*v3,int n) /* vector
    division */
   {
#if(!vectorize)
   int i;
   for(i=0;i<n;i++)
      v3[i]=v1[i]/v2[i];
#else
   __asm
      {
      push ebx
      push ecx
      push esi
      push edi
      mov  ebx,dword ptr v1
      mov  esi,dword ptr v2
      mov  edi,dword ptr v3
      mov  ecx,n
   l1:fld  qword ptr[ebx]
      fdiv qword ptr[esi]
      fstp qword ptr[edi]
      add  ebx,8
      add  esi,8
      add  edi,8
      loop l1
      pop  edi
      pop  esi
      pop  ecx
      pop  ebx
      }
#endif
   }
```

```
void vsmy(double*s,double*v1,double*v2,int n)  /* vector-
    scalar multiply */
  {
#if(!vectorize)
    int i;
    for(i=1;i<=n;i++)
      v2[i]=s*v1[i];
#else
    __asm
    {
      push ebx
      push ecx
      push esi
      push edi
      mov  ebx,dword ptr s
      mov  esi,dword ptr v1
      mov  edi,dword ptr v2
      mov  ecx,n
  l1: fld  qword ptr[esi]
      fmul qword ptr[ebx]
      fstp qword ptr[edi]
      add  esi,8
      add  edi,8
      loop l1
      pop  edi
      pop  esi
      pop  ecx
      pop  ebx
    }
#endif
  }

void vpiv(double*s,double*v1,double*v2,double*v3,int n)
    /* vector pivot */
  {
#if(!vectorize)
    int i;
    for(i=0;i<n;i++)
      v3[i]=*s*v1[i]+v2[i];
#else
    __asm
    {
      push ebx
      push ecx
      push edx
      push esi
      push edi
      mov  ebx,dword ptr s
```

```
        mov     esi,dword ptr v1
        mov     edi,dword ptr v2
        mov     edx,dword ptr v3
        mov     ecx,n
    l1: fld     qword ptr[esi]
        fmul    qword ptr[ebx]
        fadd    qword ptr[edi]
        fstp    qword ptr[edx]
        add     edx,8
        add     esi,8
        add     edi,8
        loop    l1
        pop     edi
        pop     esi
        pop     edx
        pop     ecx
        pop     ebx
        }
#endif
    }

double vdot(double*u,double*v,int n)  /* vector dot
    product */
    {
#if(!vectorize)
    int i;
    double d;
    for(d=i=0;i<n;i++)
        d+=u[i]*v[i];
    return(d);
#else
    __asm
        {
        push    ecx
        push    esi
        push    edi
        mov     esi,dword ptr u
        mov     edi,dword ptr v
        mov     ecx,n
        fldz
    l1: fld     qword ptr[esi]
        fmul    qword ptr[edi]
        faddp   st(1),st(0)
        add     esi,8
        add     edi,8
        loop    l1
        pop     edi
        pop     esi
        pop     ecx
```

```
        }
    #endif
        }
```

Consider the assembler generated by the compiler for this last procedure (see file tband.asm):

```
_vdot   proc
        fldz
        push    ebx
        mov     ebx,dword ptr _v$[esp]
        push    ebp
        push    esi
        mov     esi,dword ptr _n$[esp+8]
        xor     ebp,ebp
        cmp     esi,4
        push    edi
        mov     edi,dword ptr _u$[esp+12]
        jl      short l1
        lea     edx,dword ptr[esi-4]
        lea     ecx,dword ptr[edi+24]
        shr     edx,2
        sub     edi,ebx
        inc     edx
        lea     eax,dword ptr[ebx+8]
        lea     ebp,dword ptr[edx*4]
        fld     qword ptr[eax-8]
        add     eax,32
        fmul    qword ptr[ecx-24]
        add     ecx,32
        sub     edx,1
        faddp   st(1),st(0)
        fld     qword ptr[edi+eax-32]
        fmul    qword ptr[eax-32]
        faddp   st(1),st(0)
        fld     qword ptr[eax-24]
        fmul    qword ptr[ecx-40]
        faddp   st(1),st(0)
        fld     qword ptr[eax-16]
        fmul    qword ptr[ecx-32]
        faddp   st(1),st(0)
        jne     short $ln10@vdot
        mov     edi,dword ptr _u$[esp+12]
l1:     cmp     ebp,esi
        jge     short l3
        sub     edi,ebx
        lea     eax,dword ptr[ebx+ebp*8]
        sub     esi,ebp
l2:     fld     qword ptr[eax+edi]
        add     eax,8
```

```
            sub    esi,1
            fmul   qword ptr[eax-8]
            faddp  st(1),st(0)
            jne    short l2
    l3:     pop    edi
            pop    esi
            pop    ebp
            pop    ebx
            ret    0
    _vdot   endp
```

Compare the lines of code highlighted in red in the two preceding sections. In both cases (our compact vectorized procedure and the one created by the C compiler) there is only FLDZ instruction (loading 0.0 onto the FPU stack). The rest of the FPU instructions include FLD (load value onto FPU stack), FMUL (multiply by value), and FADDP (add value and pop FPU stack). The compact sequence contains only one of each instruction; whereas, the code generated by the C compiler (which we have just demonstrated is actually a little faster) contains 5 clusters of these three instructions. So what's up?

It's our old friend the pre-processor again. In spite of the fact that the compact instructions are very simple (for example, fld qword ptr[esi]) compared to the generated ones (for example, fld qword ptr[edi+eax-32]) this doesn't matter because the FPU never sees [edi+eax-32]. The pre-processor resolves this before passing it along. What's more, a longer sequence of operations allows the pre-processor to get up to speed, so to speak, achieving even greater overall performance. The C compiler knows this and so it encodes these repeated instructions in clusters of 4 with a separate section of 1. At runtime the cluster instructions are executed 4 at a time until there are less than 4, when it shifts over to 1 at a time. Sounds crazy? Well it should make you appreciate just how complicated it is to write a truly optimizing compiler targeting these marvelous processors and just how smart the chip developers are to think up such a device, though I suspect it worked better than they expected it to. What a nice surprise.

Chapter 12. Avoiding a Brute Force Approach

What constitutes a *brute force* approach? One example is a very fine grid Finite Difference Method (FDM) solution. This may be necessary when the problem changes rapidly over space and/or time or for part of the domain and not another. If it is only a spatial issue, you might try a highly refined grid, but this may take you so long to get right that it would be quicker to just use a large number of nodes.

Transient Diffusion: Approximate Solution

One such problem is transient diffusion, which starts with an abrupt interface, quickly changes, and then settles out to a smooth final result. If we were only doing this once, we might consider using the FDM approach, but we needed to solve this problem thousands of times. This particular remediation project involved qualifying many samples, separating them into an initially unknown number of groups, and then characterizing the groups in terms of average values with standard deviations and error bounds.

What we needed was a fast way of finding approximate solutions that could be used over-and-over again, carrying the approximations along with each sample. We were also considering granular (sandy) materials as well as amorphous (clay-like) materials. We decided to approximate the former as spherical diffusers and the latter as Cartesian. I designed the software (brute.c in the examples\brute folder) to handle all four cases: 1) FDM spherical, 2) approximate spherical, 3) FDM Cartesian, and 4) approximate Cartesian. Which case is controlled by two defines at the top of the code:

```
#define SPHERICAL
#define APPROXIMATE
#undef SPHERICAL
#undef APPROXIMATE
```

The FDM equation is defined between conditional compilation directives:

```
#ifdef SPHERICAL
dC[r]=((r+0.5)*C[r+1]-2.*r*C[r]+(r-0.5)*C[r-1])/r/dR/dR;
#else /* CARTESIAN */
dC[r]=(C[r+1]-2.*C[r]+C[r-1])/dR/dR;
#endif
```

The approximate solution uses a bisection search[34] to determine two coefficients (a and b) that best fit the sample-specific parameters:

```
#ifdef APPROXIMATE
  if(1)
    {
    int i;
    double a,a1,a2,b,b1,b2;
    a1=0.;
```

---

[34] Bisection search is a method for solving a nonlinear equation in one variable.

```
        a2=10.;
        for(i=0;i<32;i++)
          {
          a=(a1+a2)/2;
          if(cartesian(D,R,0.,a*T)>C[0])
            a1=a;
          else
            a2=a;
          }
        r=(int)(R/dR);
        b1=0.;
        b2=10.;
        for(i=0;i<32;i++)
          {
          b=(b1+b2)/2;
          if(cartesian(D,R,b*r*dR,a*T)>C[r])
            b1=b;
          else
            b2=b;
          }
        printf("%lG %lG %lG\n",2.*sqrt(D*T)/R,a,b);
        }
    #endif
```

A sample of the output is listed below:

```
solving diffusion problem
results: brute.out
0.19165 2.75847 0.97472
0.27104 1.37923 0.98216
0.33195 1.01075 0.98474
0.38331 1.00636 0.98478
0.42855 1.00424 0.98480
...
1.01413 1.00023 0.98484
1.03208 1.00022 0.98484
1.04973 1.00021 0.98484
1.06708 1.00020 0.98484
1.08415 1.00019 0.98484
...
1.56875 1.00002 0.98405
1.58041 1.00002 0.98396
1.59199 1.00001 0.98386
1.60349 1.00000 0.98375
1.61490 0.99998 0.98364
...
1.86800 0.99907 0.97743
1.87781 0.99899 0.97699
1.88757 0.99891 0.97653
1.89727 0.99882 0.97605
plot file: brute.tp2
```

Typical results for spherical (granular) geometry is shown in this figure:

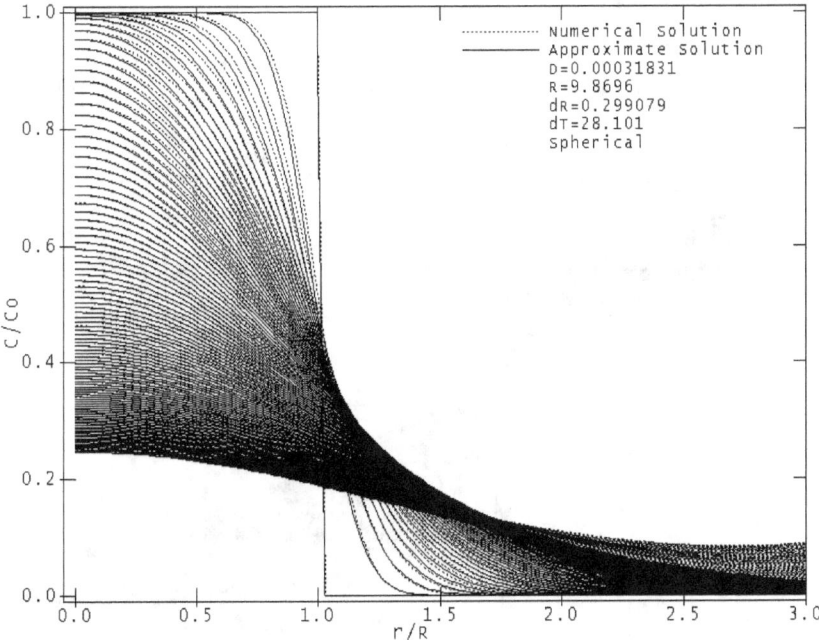

Figure 11. Spherical Solution

The approximate spherical solution (based on the complementary error function) is more than adequate.

```
double spherical(double D,double R,double r,double t)
  {
  double s;
  s=2.*sqrt(D*t)/R;
  t*=(1.131302673065950*s+0.2330227286503510)*s+1.;
  r*=(0.404882980327693*s-0.0539281549540029)*s+1.;
  return((erfc((r-R)/2./sqrt(D*t))
     -erfc((r+R)/2./sqrt(D*t)))/2.);
  }
```

Simply change the order of the four #define/#undef statements and recompile for the Cartesian case.

Typical results for the Cartesian case (amorphous) geometry is shown in this figure:

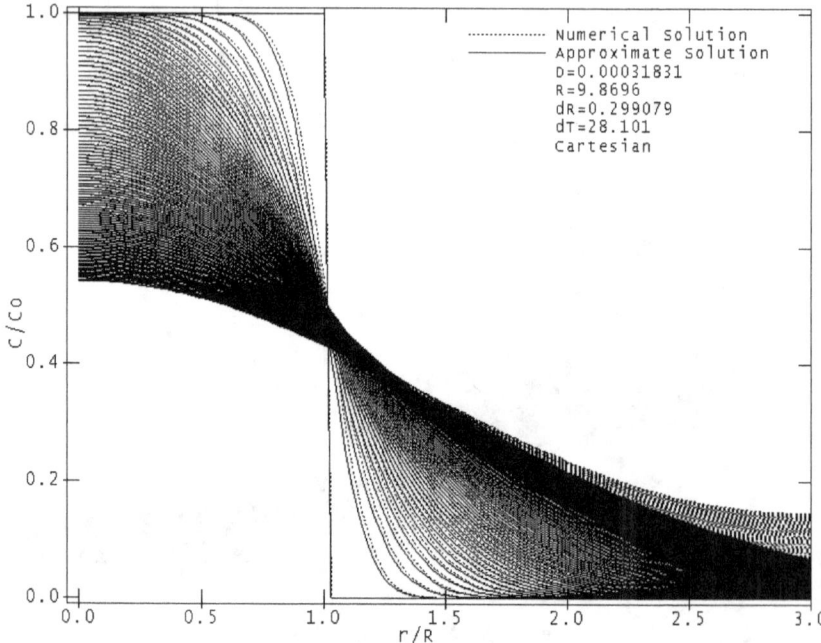

Figure 12. Cartesian Solution

The approximate Cartesian solution (also based on the complementary error function) is more than adequate.

```
double cartesian(double D,double R,double r,double t)
  {
  return((erfc((r-R)/2./sqrt(D*t))-
    erfc((r+R)/2./sqrt(D*t)))/2.);
  }
```

Approximating A Spreading Contaminant

I have provided mathematical modeling support for many remediation projects. Most of these projects have required quantifying the current situation, including how much contaminant is present and where. One early project (before I developed more sophisticated methods) began with the concept of using the Finite Difference Method (FDM) to represent the field and then add up the concentration at all of the nodes to arrive at a total contaminant mass. At first we thought it would be adequate to use 100×100×100, which meant one million nodes. We were able to manage this with the available hardware, but the uncertainty was too great when we considered that the concentration varied by orders of magnitude. After further consideration we settled on a 400×400×400 grid, which was 64 million nodes and beyond the hardware capability. We considered other options but funds and time were limited and so we took a different approach.

Just as a Fast Fourier Transform (FFT) can be used to approximate and resolve a Computer Aided Tomography (CAT) scan, other orthogonal functions can be used to approximate fields. The advantage of this approach is that additional terms (and increased accuracy) can be added with very little extra computational effort, unlike solving a FDM model, which increases computationally with the cube of the number of nodes (not cubed because it's 3D but cubed because it involves solving a matrix, which increases roughly with the cube of the number of unknowns or equations).

Hermite polynomials are ideal for approximating a contaminant field because they are orthogonal over the infinite domain (-∞ to +∞). Hermite polynomials satisfy several differential equations, two of which are given below:

$$\frac{d^2y}{dx^2} + 2x\frac{dy}{dx} + 2ny = 0 \quad y = \sum CnHn(x) \quad (12.1)$$

$$\frac{d^2y}{dx^2} + (2n+1-x^2)y = 0 \quad y = \sum CnHn(x)e^{\frac{-x^2}{2}} \quad (12.2)$$

Hermite polynomials are orthogonal with respect to the weighting function exp($-x^2/2$) over the doubly infinite range as indicated by the following integral:

$$\int_{-\infty}^{+\infty} Hn(x)Hm(x)e^{-x^2}dx = \begin{cases} \sqrt{\pi}2^n n! & if\ (n=m) \\ 0 & if\ (n \neq m) \end{cases} \quad (12.3)$$

Terms in the series are computed from the orthogonality conditions:

$$Cn = \frac{\int_{-\infty}^{+\infty} F(x)Hn(x)e^{-x^2}dx}{\int_{-\infty}^{+\infty} H_n^2(x)e^{-x^2}dx} \quad (12.4)$$

A test of the integration methods follows by applying the technique to the orthogonality condition (Equation 12.3). If you generate a sequence of data sets, which are the various products of the Hermite functions, the accuracy of the integration technique can be determined by checking the residual matrix whose elements are defined as follows:

$$Rn = \frac{\int_{-\infty}^{+\infty} Hn(x)Hm(x)e^{-x^2}dx}{\int_{-\infty}^{+\infty} H_n^2(x)e^{-x^2}dx} \quad (12.5)$$

The diagonal elements will be one and the off-diagonal elements should be much smaller than one. In order to extend this method to 2 or 3 dimensions it is only necessary to define the series of products of the one-dimensional Hermite polynomials as indicated below:

$$\int_{-\infty}^{+\infty}\int_{-\infty}^{+\infty}\int_{-\infty}^{+\infty} Hn(x)Hm(x)e^{(-x^2-y^2-z^2)}dxdydz$$
$$= \begin{cases} \neq 0 \text{ if } (n = m) \\ = 0 \text{ if } (n \neq m) \end{cases} \quad (12.6)$$

The first 6 Hermite polynomials are shown below:

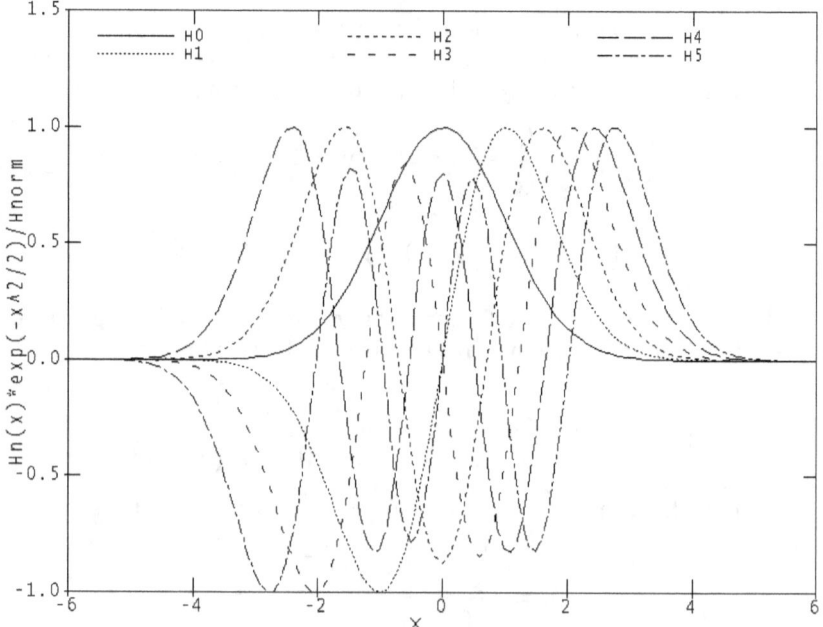

Figure 13. First Six Hermite Polynomials

We add terms, calculate the sum, evaluate the uncertainty, and end when the project criteria are satisfied.

A typical sequence of approximations for 1D is shown in this next figure:

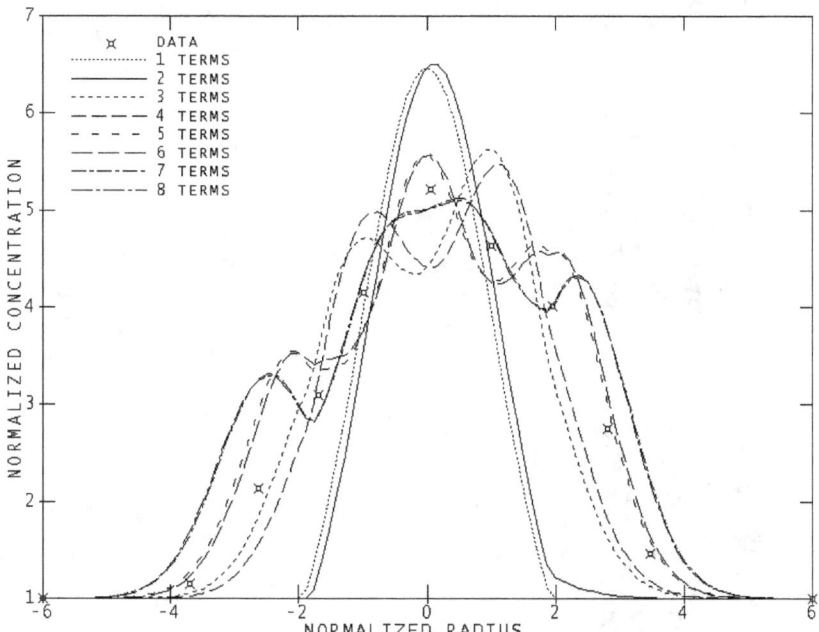

Figure 14. Typical 8-Term Approximation

Slices through a typical 3D field are shown in this next figure:

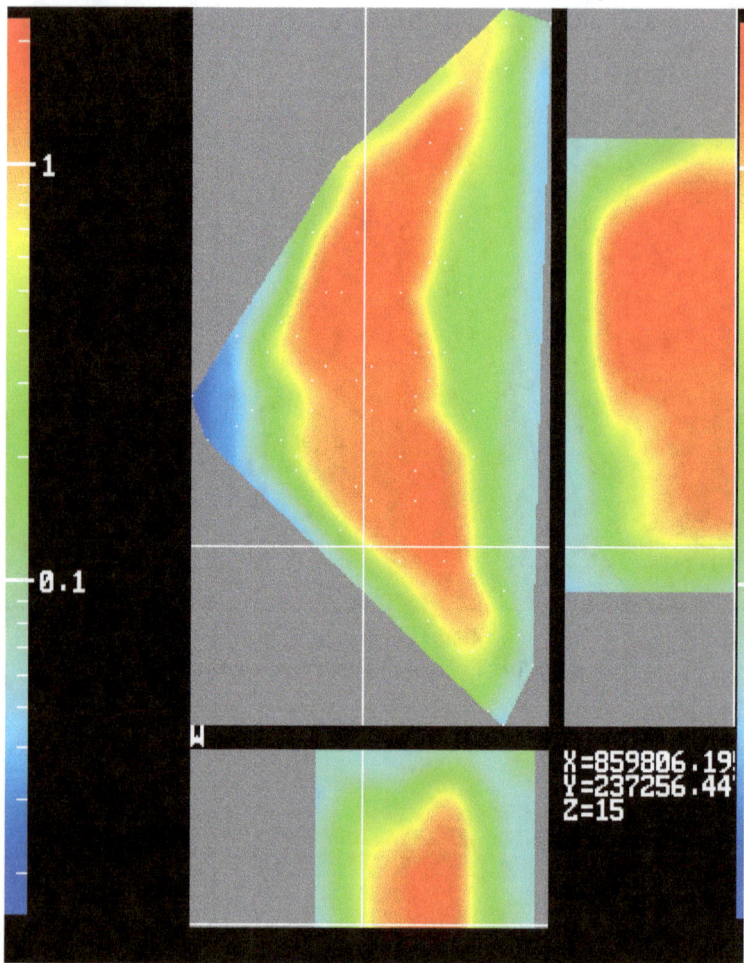

Figure 15. Slices Through A Typical 3D Field

<u>Approximating Magnetometer Data</u>

A similar problem having a different spatial behavior; that is, not inherently fading away with increasing distance, is obtained with a magnetometer. The calculation is almost the same, as is the motivation. Instead of seeking to characterize a contaminant field without an unwieldy number of nodes, we seek to identify buried debris, in this particular case unexploded ordinance. A brave (or very daring) technician scans the area with a magnetometer, digitally recording the data, then brings it back to the trailer for analysis. After imaging the results, a plan to dig up the device is formulated. This plan will depend on the nature of the device, which will be determined from the size and shape. The software I developed for this purpose runs quickly on any laptop, allowing the entire process to be performed on site, rather than taking the data back to the office for analysis. A typical map is shown below:

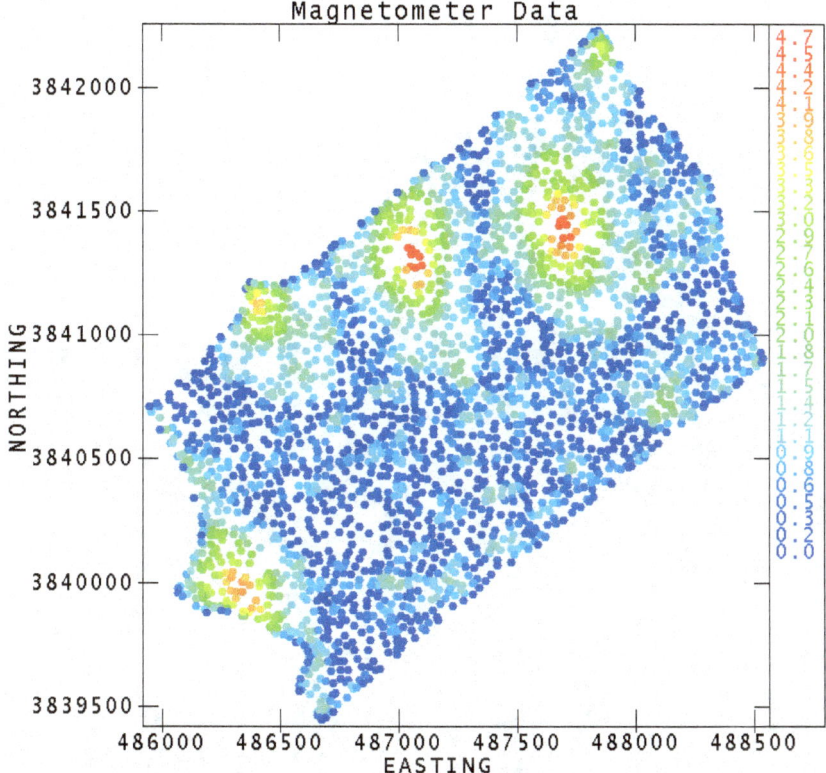

Figure 16. Magnetometer Data (Before Analysis)

Many more such examples plus free software and sample data files can be found in my book, *The Many Uses of Orthogonal Functions*,
https://www.amazon.com/dp/B07GT8TLDV

Chapter 13. Fast Fourier Transform

The Fast Fourier Transform (FFT) is perhaps the oldest mathematical trick used to simplify what would otherwise be a much more computationally-intensive task. This approach has been so useful in such field as Computer Aided Tomography (CAT) scanning, that specialized hardware was developed just for this purpose, even in the very early days of computers. We have already explored two types of orthogonal functions (Hermite and Legendre) in the previous chapter. The FFT is based on the orthogonality relationship of the sine and cosine. There are numerous articles on the Web about FFT, so we won't dwell on the theoretical aspects here, only the actual number crunching.

To illustrate we begin with some familiar sounds: touch tone phone beeps. If you research this topic on the Web you will discover that these familiar sounds are actually a combination of two or more distinct pure tones. If we were to perform an FFT on these we should see only a few terms. You will find a small program (wav2fft.c) in folder examples\wav2fft that reads a WAV file and performs an FFT. This is what it produces...

```
wav2fft tone1.wav
    i      c[i]       s[i]
   70   -0.40198    0.05332
  121   -0.43863    0.18254
wav2fft tone4.wav
    i      c[i]       s[i]
   70   -0.40198    0.05332
  121   -0.43863    0.18254
wav2fft tone6.wav
    i      c[i]       s[i]
   77   -0.25353    0.41987
  148   -0.35521   -0.16017
wav2fft tone7.wav
    i      c[i]       s[i]
   77   -0.25448    0.41885
  121   -0.43660    0.18266
wav2fft tone9.wav
    i      c[i]       s[i]
   85    0.01339    0.47168
  148   -0.35452   -0.16206
```

There are some additional harmonics in the other keys. All of the tones can be found in this same folder. The point is that we can decompose a signal or similar data into its underlying components using this method. The core code for the FFT in this C program is:

```
for(i=0;i<m;i++)
  {
  ci=cj=cos(2*i*M_PI/n);
  si=sj=sin(2*i*M_PI/n);
  for(c[i]=s[i]=cc=ss=j=0;j<n;j++)
```

```c
    {
    c[i]+=cj*f[j];
    s[i]+=sj*f[j];
    cc+=cj*cj;
    ss+=sj*sj;
    ck=ci*cj-si*sj;
    sk=si*cj+ci*sj;
    cj=ck;
    sj=sk;
    }
c[i]/=cc;
if(i)
    s[i]/=ss;
}
```

There is only a slight difference in handling the sine and cosine terms owing to the zeroth cosine term being 1. You will find a similar program (FFT.FOR) written in F90 in the folder examples\FFT. The same section of F90 code is:

```
DO J=1,M
    T=2.*PI*(X(J)-XMIN)/(XMAX-XMIN)
    YJ=Y(J)
    C0=1.
    FY(1)=FY(1)+C0*YJ
    FF(1)=FF(1)+C0*C0
    C1=COS(T)
    S1=SIN(T)
    FY(2)=FY(2)+S1*YJ
    FF(2)=FF(2)+S1*S1
    FY(3)=FY(3)+C1*YJ
    FF(3)=FF(3)+C1*C1
    C=C1
    S=S1
    DO I=4,N,2
       Q=C1*C-S1*S
       S=C1*S+S1*C
       C=Q
       FY(I)=FY(I)+S*YJ
       FF(I)=FF(I)+S*S
       K=I+1
         IF(K.LE.N)THEN
            FY(K)=FY(K)+C*YJ
            FF(K)=FF(K)+C*C
         ENDIF
    ENDDO
ENDDO
DO I=1,N
   FY(I)=FY(I)/FF(I)
ENDDO
```

A sample of program output for the data file found in this folder is:

```
FASTFT/V1.0: Fast Fourier Transform
data points read=204
time ranges from 6.68333 to 2713.35
head ranges from 0.5 to 14.6
determining Fast Fourier Transform
Fast Fourier Transform
freq  component
  0   1.000000
  1   0.344532
  2   0.151178
 ...  ........
 50   0.005423
```

Both of these compilers (C and F90) produce an assembler listing (wav2fft.asm and FFT.asm) that can be found in these same folders. While the loops above can be implemented in assembler and some speed increase may result, it is not likely, considering the previous examples and how the pre-processors work. Instead, we consider the case in which there are far more data points than terms in the Fourier series. This is often true and when it is, if we were to express this problem in terms of a rectangular matrix, it would have far more rows than columns. The preceding loops process the matrix by rows. If there were far more rows than columns and we were instead to process the matrix by columns, it would be more suited to using the VIS described previously and that is exactly what we will consider next. This vectorizable implementation can be found in FFTVIS.FOR in the examples\FFT folder. As can be seen from the following code, the vectorized implementation is quite different. The comments explain each step.

```
      SUBROUTINE VISFFT(X,Y,NX,C1,CN,S1,SN,FX,W1,W2,W3,
     &W4,F,NF)
      IMPLICIT INTEGER*4(I-N),REAL*8(A-H,O-Z)
      DIMENSION
     X(1),Y(1),C1(1),CN(1),S1(1),SN(1),FX(1),W1(1),W2(1),
     &W3(1),W4(1),F(1)
      DO I=1,NX
        C1(I)=COS(X(I))
        S1(I)=SIN(X(I))
      ENDDO
      CALL VMOV(C1,1,CN,1,NX)
      CALL VMOV(S1,1,SN,1,NX)
C
COMPUTE F(1) BY PROJECTING Y ONTO COS(0) AND NORMALIZE
C
      CALL VDOT(CY,1.,0,Y,1,NX)
      CC=FLOAT(NX)
      F(1)=CY/CC
C
```

```
COMPUTE THE NEW RESIDUAL BY FX=Y-F(1)*COS(0)
C
      CALL VPIV(-F(1),1.,0,Y,1,FX,1,NX)
C
COMPUTE F(2) BY PROJECTING FX ONTO SIN(X) AND NORMALIZE
C
      CALL VDOT(SF,S1,1,FX,1,NX)
      CALL VDOT(SS,S1,1,S1,1,NX)
      F(2)=SF/SS
C
COMPUTE THE NEW RESIDUAL BY FX=FX-F(2)*SIN(X)
C
      CALL VPIV(-F(2),S1,1,FX,1,FX,1,NX)
C
COMPUTE F(3) BY PROJECTING FX ONTO COS(X) AND NORMALIZE
C
      CALL VDOT(CF,C1,1,FX,1,NX)
      CALL VDOT(CC,C1,1,C1,1,NX)
      F(3)=CF/CC
C
COMPUTE THE NEW RESIDUAL BY FX=FX-F(3)*COS(X)
C
      CALL VPIV(-F(3),C1,1,FX,1,FX,1,NX)
      IF(NF.LE.3)GOTO 300
      N=3
C
C USE ANGLE SUM FORMULA TO GET NEXT 2 TERMS IN SERIES
C SIN(A+B)=SIN(A)*COS(B)+COS(A)*SIN(B)
C COS(A+B)=COS(A)*COS(B)-SIN(A)*SIN(B)
C
  200 CALL VMPY(SN,1,C1,1,W1,1,NX)
      CALL VMPY(S1,1,CN,1,W2,1,NX)
      CALL VMPY(CN,1,C1,1,W3,1,NX)
      CALL VMPY(SN,1,S1,1,W4,1,NX)
      CALL VADD(W1,1,W2,1,SN,1,NX)
      CALL VSUB(W3,1,W4,1,CN,1,NX)
C
COMPUTE "F(2N+1)" BY PROJECTING "FX" ONTO "SIN(NX)" AND
   NORMALIZING
C
      CALL VDOT(SF,SN,1,FX,1,NX)
      CALL VDOT(SS,SN,1,SN,1,NX)
      N=N+1
      F(N)=SF/SS
C
C COMPUTE THE NEW RESIDUAL BY "FX=FX-F(2N+1)*SIN(NX)"
C
      CALL VPIV(-F(N),SN,1,FX,1,FX,1,NX)
      IF(N.GE.NF)GOTO 300
```

```
C
C   COMPUTE "F(2N+2)" BY PROJECTING "FX" ONTO "COS(NX)"
    AND NORMALIZING
C
      CALL VDOT(CF,CN,1,FX,1,NX)
      CALL VDOT(CC,CN,1,CN,1,NX)
      N=N+1
      F(N)=CF/CC
C
C   COMPUTE THE NEW RESIDUAL BY "FX=FX-F(2N+2)*COS(NX)"
C
      CALL VPIV(-F(N),CN,1,FX,1,FX,1,NX)
      IF(N.GE.NF)GOTO 300
      GOTO 200
C
C   COMPUTE TRANSFORM "Y" BY "FX=Y-FX"
C
  300 CALL VSUB(Y,1,FX,1,FX,1,NX)
C
      RETURN
      END
```

Chapter 14. Romberg vs. Gauss

Continuing with the theme of working smarter, not harder, we turn to numerical integration. A colleague once said to me, "I can get whatever accuracy I want by using Romberg's Method." To which I responded, "So can I using Gauss Quadrature, only faster." There are many articles on the Web describing Romberg's Method[35], which can be stated:

$$h_n = \frac{1}{2^n}(b-a) \quad (14.1)$$

where h is the interval, while a and b are the lower and upper limits of the integral. The integral becomes:

$$R(0,0) = h_1(f(b) + f(a)) \quad (14.2)$$

where $f(a)$ and $f(b)$ are the function evaluated at a and b, respectively. Higher order terms are defined:

$$R(n,0) = \frac{1}{2}R(n-1,0) + h_n \sum_{k=1}^{2^{n-1}} f(a + (2k-1)h_n) \quad (14.3)$$

and by:

$$R(n,m) = \frac{1}{4^m - 1}(4^m R(n, m-1) - R(n-1, m-1)) \quad (14.4)$$

The implementation is listed below and can be found in the online archive in folder examples\intest in file intest.c:

```
double Romberg(double F(double),double X1,double X2,int
    n)
{
int i,i1,j,j1,jj;
double dX,E,H,H2,S,X;
static double R[15][15];
dX=X2-X1;
H=dX;
R[0][0]=(F(X1)+F(X2))*H/2.;
if(n<2)
   return(R[0][0]);
jj=1;
i1=0;
for(i=1;i<n;i++)
```

---

[35] Romberg, W., "Vereinfachte Numerische Integration (Simplified Numerical Integration)", Det Kongelige Norske Videnskabers Selskab Forhandlinger (Transactions of the Royal Norwegian Society of Sciences), Trondheim, Vol. 28, No. 7, pp. 30–36, 1955.

```
    {
    H2=H/2.;
    X=X1-H2;
    for(S=j=0;j<jj;j++)
        {
        X+=H;
        S+=F(X);
        }
    R[i][0]=(R[i1][0]+H*S)/2.;
    H=H2;
    for(j1=0,E=j=1;j<=i;j++)
        {
        E*=4.;
        R[i][j]=(E*R[i][j1]-R[i1][j1])/(E-1.);
        j1=j;
        }
    jj+=jj;
    i1=i;
    }
return(R[n-1][n-1]);
}
```

Gauss Quadrature[36] can be expressed by the following formula:

$$\int_a^b f(y)dy = \left(\frac{b-a}{2}\right)\sum_{i=1}^n w_i f(y_i)$$
$$y_i = \left(\frac{b-a}{2}\right)x_i + \left(\frac{b+a}{2}\right)$$
(14.5)

where w_i and x_i are the weights and abscissas, respectively. Each order of Gauss Quadrature is different; for example, the 4-point method is listed below:

```
double Gauss4(double F(double),double X1,double X2)
    {
    short int i;
    double dX,G,aX;
    static double A[]={0.339981043585,0.861136311594};
    static double W[]={0.652145154863,0.347854845137};
    dX=(X2-X1)/2.;
    aX=(X1+X2)/2.;
    for(G=i=0;i<2;i++)
        G+=W[i]*(F(aX-dX*A[i])+F(aX+dX*A[i]));
    G*=dX;
    return(G);
    }
```

---

[36] cf. Abramowitz & Stegun *Handbook of Mathematical Functions*

We now compare these two methods by integrating some function for which we know the analytical result. This allows us to calculate the error for each method and ultimately the number of digits of accuracy achieved by each method, which can then be divided by the runtime to obtain a measure of the efficiency.

```
INTEST/V2.02: test methods for numerical integration
method                error              µsec      digit/µs
3-point Romberg       0.438323997915045  0.000001   246579
5-point Romberg       0.083115335609608  0.000002   449814
9-point Romberg       0.011042827074904  0.000004   441948
17-point Romberg      0.000829884340796  0.000008   375196
33-point Romberg      0.000030076496687  0.000016   283903
65-point Romberg      0.000000465695660  0.000033   190370
129-point Romberg     0.000000002818299  0.000064   134220
257-point Romberg     0.000000000006244  0.000128    87197
513-point Romberg     0.000000000000004  0.000241    59934
1025-point Romberg    0.000000000000002  0.000494    29887
2049-point Romberg    0.000000000000010  0.000978    14331
4097-point Romberg    0.000000000000003  0.001968     7405
8193-point Romberg    0.000000000000021  0.003904     3502
16385-point Romberg   0.000000000000020  0.007833     1750
2-point Gauss         0.196202114270641  0.000001   743335
3-point Gauss         0.055975349146734  0.000001   846064
4-point Gauss         0.015615569121244  0.000002   946602
5-point Gauss         0.004301982256929  0.000002   974728
6-point Gauss         0.001177008886287  0.000003  1015818
7-point Gauss         0.000320744705316  0.000003  1079810
8-point Gauss         0.000087190961628  0.000004  1085963
9-point Gauss         0.000023663626913  0.000004  1035371
10-point Gauss        0.000006415107776  0.000005  1061738
12-point Gauss        0.000000470415039  0.000006  1114977
16-point Gauss        0.000000002511189  0.000008  1127638
20-point Gauss        0.000000000015010  0.000009  1142678
40-point Gauss        0.000000000001342  0.000019   629792
96-point Gauss        0.000000000000003  0.000045   320391
```

We see from this table that the Romberg method reaches it's peak efficiency (about 400K digits/µs) at 5- to 9-point then falls off rapidly. The accuracy improves (e.g., error≈0.000000000000020), but the time required to achieve that accuracy does not improve. This is because the order of the Romberg method does not increase with additional points, only the interval decreases. Each case for Gauss Quadrature not only involves more points (viz., x_i) but also increasing order of accuracy. In fact, Gauss Quadrature is the only method that increases in order of accuracy faster than the number of points increases. This is why using Gauss Quadrature over Romberg illustrates working *smarter*, not *harder*. Many more such details can be found in my book, *Numerical Calculus*.

https://www.amazon.com/dp/B07BS1DN1S

Chapter 15. Predictor/Corrector vs. Runge-Kutta

A similar situation (working smarter, not harder) carries over from numerical integration to the solution of differential equations. While no one ever specifically told me that they could achieve any level of accuracy with a predictor/corrector scheme, it would seem from their implementations that this was presumed. Just like Romberg, predictor/corrector schemes work quite well but are not the fastest way of solving differential equations.

The predictor/corrector approach we will consider is Milne's Method[37], which is said to have a truncation order of $O(h^5)$, where h is the step size.

$$P \quad y_{n+1} = y_{n-3} + \frac{4h}{3}\left(2y'_n - y'_{n-1} + 2y'_{n-2}\right)$$
$$C \quad y_{n+1} = y_{n-1} + \frac{h}{3}\left(y'_{n-1} + 4y'_n + y'_{n+1}\right) \tag{15.1}$$

For comparison, we select the Runge-Kutta Method[38] having the same truncation order; that is, 4th order, which can be expressed:

$$y_{n+1} = y_n + \frac{k_1}{6} + \frac{k_2}{3} + \frac{k_3}{3} + \frac{k_4}{6}$$
$$k_1 = hf(x_n, y_n)$$
$$k_2 = hf\left(x_n + \frac{h}{2}, y_n + \frac{k_1}{2}\right) \tag{15.2}$$
$$k_3 = hf\left(x_n + \frac{h}{2}, y_n + \frac{k_2}{2}\right)$$
$$k_4 = hf(x_n + h, y_n + k_3)$$

Something rarely discussed in textbooks in the context of Milne's Method is just how are we supposed to get this thing started? The first step (n+1) requires four previous values (n, n-1, n-2, and n-3)! Of course, Runge-Kutta poses no such problem. We're hoping to compare the accuracy and efficiency of these two methods, so for the purposes of our investigation, we will allow Milne to utilize RK for the first four steps.

We must select a test problem that has an analytical solution so that we can compare accuracy. We want to select a challenging problem and not a trivial one. A somewhat challenging ODE is:

---

[37] Milne, W. E., "A Note on the Numerical Integration of Differential Equations," *NBS Journal of Research*, Vol. 43, pp. 537-542, 1949.
[38] cf. Abramowitz & Stegun *Handbook of Mathematical Functions*

$$\frac{dy}{dx} = \frac{y}{\sqrt{x}} \tag{15.3}$$

The solution is:

$$y = e^{2\sqrt{x}} \tag{15.4}$$

and is shown in the following figure:

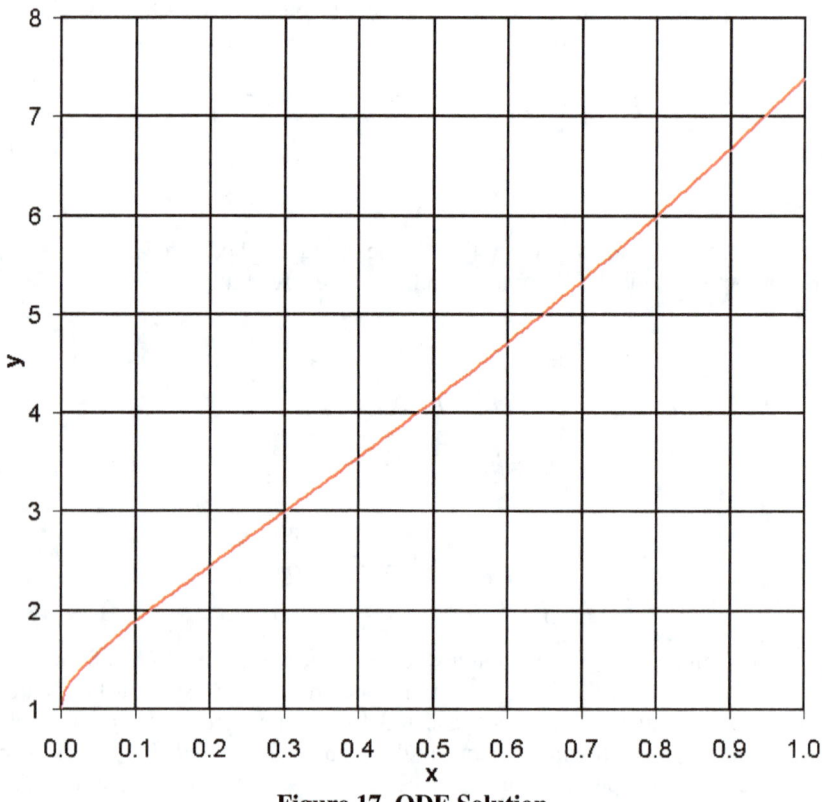

Figure 17. ODE Solution

The slope is infinite at $x=0$ and this is intentional to make the problem challenging. The code (milne.c) can be found in the online archive in the folder examples\Milne. The error vs. step size (h) and runtime vs. error for 4th Order Runge-Kutta are shown in the following figures:

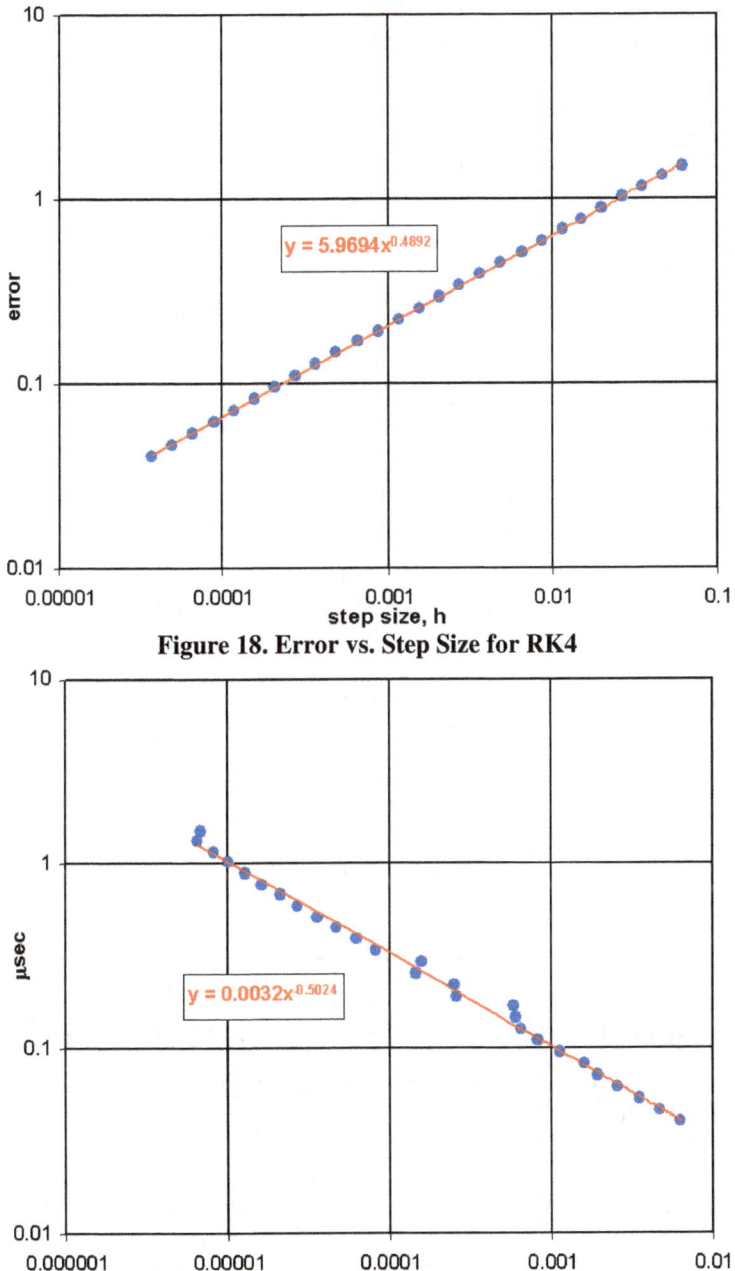

Figure 18. Error vs. Step Size for RK4

Figure 19. Runtime vs. Error for RK4

We see highly desirable (even ideal) behavior in both of these figures. In the first figure, error is essentially proportional to the square root of step size, $h^{0.5}$, which means smaller step size = smaller error. In the second figure runtime is inversely proportional to the square root of error, which means smaller error = more runtime but not unreasonably so. Milne's Method being a predictor/corrector approach has two variables: 1) step size and 2) number of corrector steps. The error vs. step size for 1 to 6 correction steps is shown in this next figure:

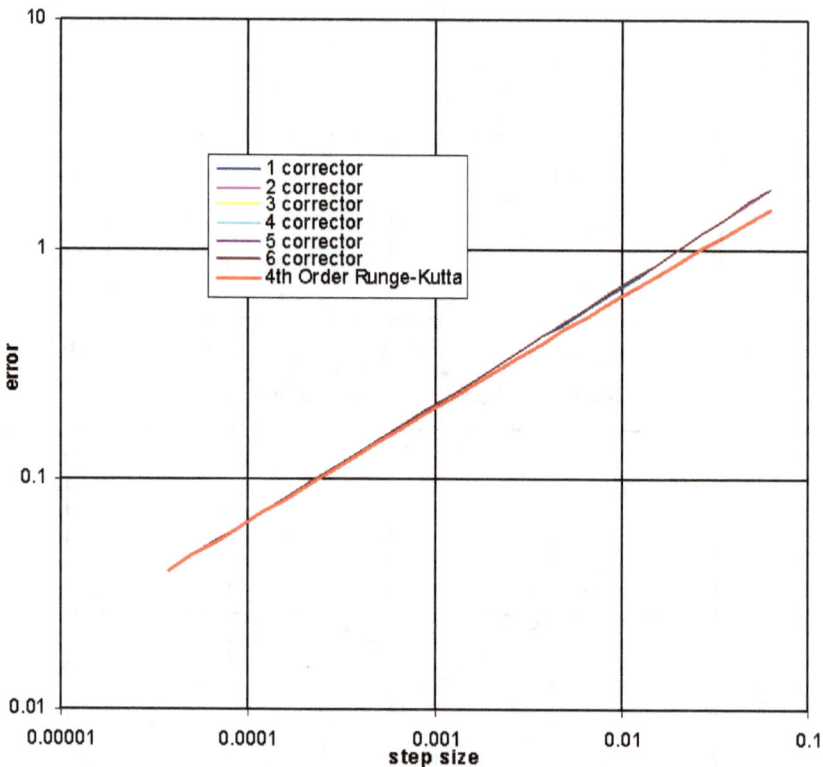

Figure 20. Error vs. Step Size for RK4 and Milne's Method

In this figure we see that the number of corrector steps has no visible impact on the error. This is something I point out in both texts, *Numerical Calculus* and *Differential Equations*. Predictor/corrector (and error control methods) sound good in theory but rarely deliver in practice. As I have provided the source code for each example, you're welcome to try these techniques out on your own problems. This is a phenomenon I have observed for many years. Many papers have been published "demonstrating" how effective one approach or another is. What these authors often fail to explain is how much time they devoted to crafting an example that proved their point.

This next figure shows the runtime vs. error for both methods.

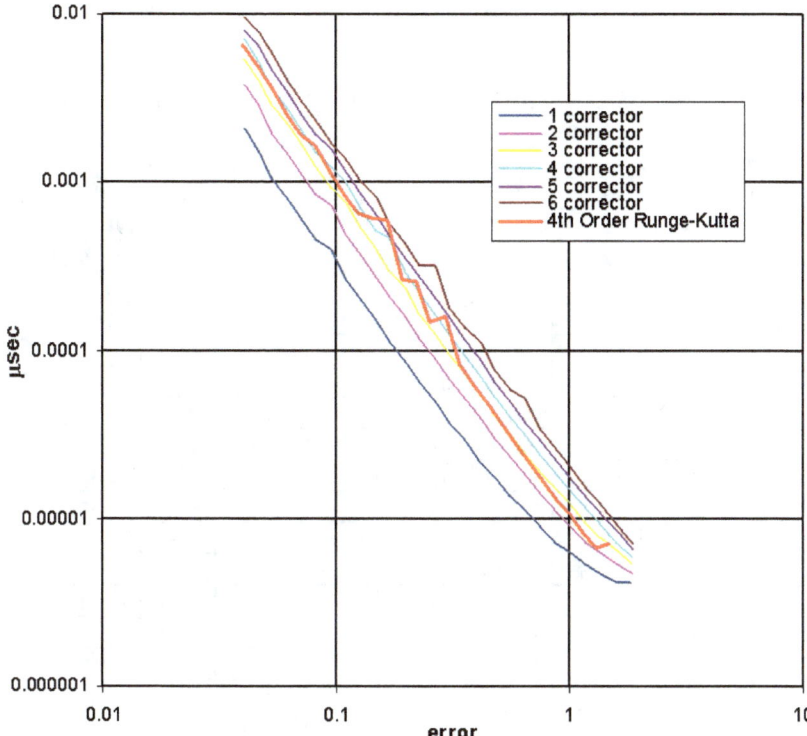

Figure 21. Runtime vs. Error for RK4 and Milne's Method

In this figure we see that RK4 is right in the middle of the grouping, requiring about the same time as 3 corrector steps, which should be obvious from comparing Equations 15.1 and 15.2. So how then can we compare the efficiency of these methods? One way would be to divide by the error (smaller is better) and also the runtime (quicker is better). These results are listed in the following table.

Table 15.1 Method Efficiency

step		Ranking=1/error/msec					
		Milne's Method Correction Steps					
h	RK4	1	2	3	4	5	6
0.0625000	95,929	129,871	113,540	**101,550**	**91,877**	**83,887**	**77,176**
0.0476190	**113,101**	149,970	117,476	97,020	85,825	71,982	67,619
0.0357143	103,316	154,430	**118,331**	92,950	78,866	68,488	60,525
0.0270270	95,390	160,129	116,192	88,836	73,668	62,925	54,916
0.0204082	85,703	**160,528**	109,638	81,579	67,459	57,506	49,407
0.0153846	76,761	157,720	101,898	75,471	61,748	51,587	44,298
0.0116279	68,370	148,572	94,513	69,487	55,590	45,875	39,376
0.0087719	61,510	137,774	85,640	62,279	49,374	40,899	29,308
0.0065790	52,875	130,683	76,775	55,894	43,944	35,999	30,634
0.0049505	46,231	117,828	69,075	49,602	38,694	31,719	26,778
0.0037175	40,454	107,591	61,262	43,534	34,033	27,755	21,603
0.0027933	35,281	95,929	54,332	38,388	29,768	24,309	20,542
0.0020964	21,121	86,269	47,636	33,706	26,022	20,295	17,817
0.0015723	26,555	76,125	41,890	29,433	22,764	18,533	11,589
0.0011793	17,424	66,893	36,604	25,719	19,825	15,687	13,594
0.0008850	19,651	58,514	31,956	21,419	17,254	14,039	11,626
0.0006640	9,887	51,329	27,855	19,503	12,374	12,200	10,147
0.0004980	11,143	44,795	24,236	16,383	13,046	10,402	8,100
0.0003736	11,912	39,025	21,085	14,527	11,187	9,126	7,685
0.0002802	10,721	34,017	18,327	11,698	9,070	7,939	6,631
0.0002102	9,171	25,804	14,253	11,027	8,477	6,529	6,159
0.0001576	7,423	26,637	14,384	9,594	7,970	6,295	5,113
0.0001182	7,245	23,488	12,604	8,243	6,778	5,525	4,645
0.0000887	6,276	20,300	10,996	7,240	5,901	4,737	3,997
0.0000665	5,255	17,777	9,529	6,480	5,096	3,995	3,219
0.0000499	4,464	14,461	7,549	5,199	4,083	3,336	2,784
0.0000374	3,847	12,036	6,573	4,621	3,498	3,116	2,618

The largest value in each column is shown in bold. RK4 is the second one down, 1-step corrector Milne's is the fifth down, 2-step Milne's is the third down, and the rest (3-step through 6-step) become less effective with each decrease in step size, which is essential for accuracy, making this method much less attractive than RK4. Also, don't forget that we had to use RK4 just to get Milne's method started, so why would anyone use Milne's method other than as an illustration or for historical interest? Beats me... Again, if you want to make best use of computing hardware, then work *smarter*, not *harder* and know your algorithms.

Chapter 16. Implicit vs. Explicit Methods

Implicit methods are generally more computationally intensive and also more difficult to implement. In this chapter we will compare two explicit and two implicit methods. The explicit methods are forward Euler and 2nd Order Runge-Kutta. The forward (explicit) Euler method is:

$$y_{n+1} = y_n + hf(x_n, y_n) \qquad (16.1)$$

and is implemented thus:

```
double ExplicitEuler(double L,double*x,double*y,int
    steps)
{
int s;
double h;
h=L/(steps-1);
x[0]=0.;
y[0]=exact(x[0]);
for(s=1;s<steps;s++)
    {
    x[s]=x[s-1]+h;
    y[s]=y[s-1]+h*dydx(x[s-1],y[s-1]);
    }
return(fabs(y[steps-1]-exact(x[steps-1])));
```

The 2nd Order Runge-Kutta is:

$$y_{n+1} = y_n + \frac{k_1 + k_2}{2}$$
$$k_1 = hf(x_n, y_n) \qquad (16.2)$$
$$k_2 = hf(x_n + h, y_n + k_1)$$

and is implemented thus:

```
double RungeKutta2(double L,double*x,double*y,int steps)
{
int s;
double h,k1,k2;
h=L/(steps-1);
x[0]=0.;
y[0]=exact(x[0]);
for(s=1;s<steps;s++)
    {
    x[s]=x[s-1]+h;
    k1=dydx(x[s-1],y[s-1]);
    k2=dydx(x[s],y[s-1]+h*k1);
    y[s]=y[s-1]+h*(k1+k2)/2.;
    }
return(fabs(y[steps-1]-exact(x[steps-1])));
```

The two implicit methods are backward Euler and Crank-Nicolson. The backward Euler is:

$$y_{n+1} = y_n + hf(x_{n+1}, y_{n+1}) \tag{16.3}$$

and is implemented thus:

```
double ImplicitEuler(double L,double*x,double*y,int
   steps,int corrections)
{
int c,s;
double h;
h=L/(steps-1);
x[0]=0.;
y[0]=exact(x[0]);
for(s=1;s<steps;s++)
  {
  x[s]=x[s-1]+h;
  y[s]=y[s-1]+h*dydx(x[s-1],y[s-1]);
  for(c=1;c<corrections;c++)
    y[s]=y[s-1]+h*dydx(x[s],y[s]);
  }
return(fabs(y[steps-1]-exact(x[steps-1])));
```

As the y_{n+1} term appears on both sides of this equation, the method requires iterative solution. You can iterate and check the difference or simply iterate several times. Either way produces much the same results for most problems.

The Crank-Nicolson method can be stated:

$$y_{n+1} = y_n + \frac{h}{2}[f(x_n, y_n) + f(x_{n+1}, y_{n+1})] \tag{16.4}$$

For an ODE this can be implemented in the same way as the backward Euler. For a PDE, this involves repetitive solution of a matrix. Here it is implemented thus:

```
double CrankNicolson(double L,double*x,double*y,int
   steps,int corrections)
{
int c,s;
double dy1,dy2,h;
h=L/(steps-1);
x[0]=0.;
y[0]=exact(x[0]);
for(s=1;s<steps;s++)
  {
  x[s]=x[s-1]+h;
  dy1=dydx(x[s-1],y[s-1]);
  y[s]=y[s-1]+h*dy1;
  for(c=1;c<corrections;c++)
    {
```

```
    dy2=dydx(x[s],y[s]);
    y[s]=y[s-1]+h*(dy1+dy2)/2.;
    }
  }
  return(fabs(y[steps-1]-exact(x[steps-1])));
```

We will compare these methods for two problems using the same code (crank.c) located in folder examples\crank. The first problem we will investigate is given by the following ODE:

$$\frac{dy}{dx} = y\cos(x) \tag{16.5}$$

The analytical solution is:

$$y = e^{\sin(x)} \tag{16.6}$$

The numerical solutions for *x=0 to 50* using 1000 steps is shown below:

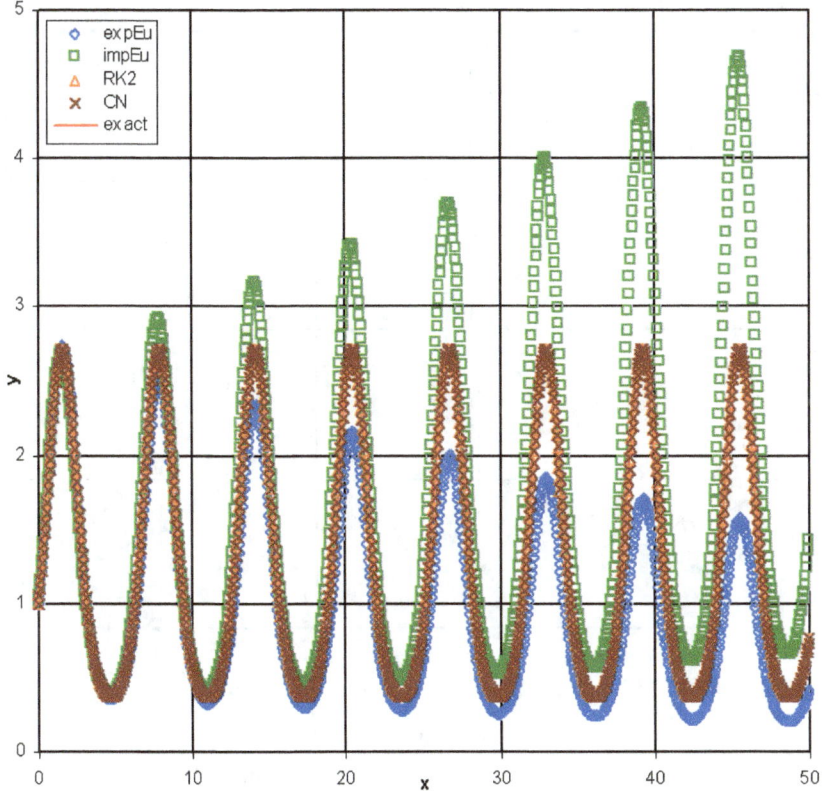

Figure 22. Numerical Solutions to First Problem

The RK2 and CN solutions are on top of the exact; however, both the explicit (forward blue) and implicit (backward green) Euler methods depart from the exact solution. The forward Euler departs because it lacks higher order terms; while the backward Euler departs because it over-emphasizes the higher order terms. Neither one is ever recommended. Even RK2 is adequate for this problem. CN is simple enough to implement in this case, but not for PDEs, as the matrix calculations grow with order n^3, where n is the number of variables. It is a rare problem for which Runge-Kutta methods are not optimal. Many examples in the literature cautioning against RK are specifically formulated to showcase the performance of arcane algorithms. An exploded view is shown below:

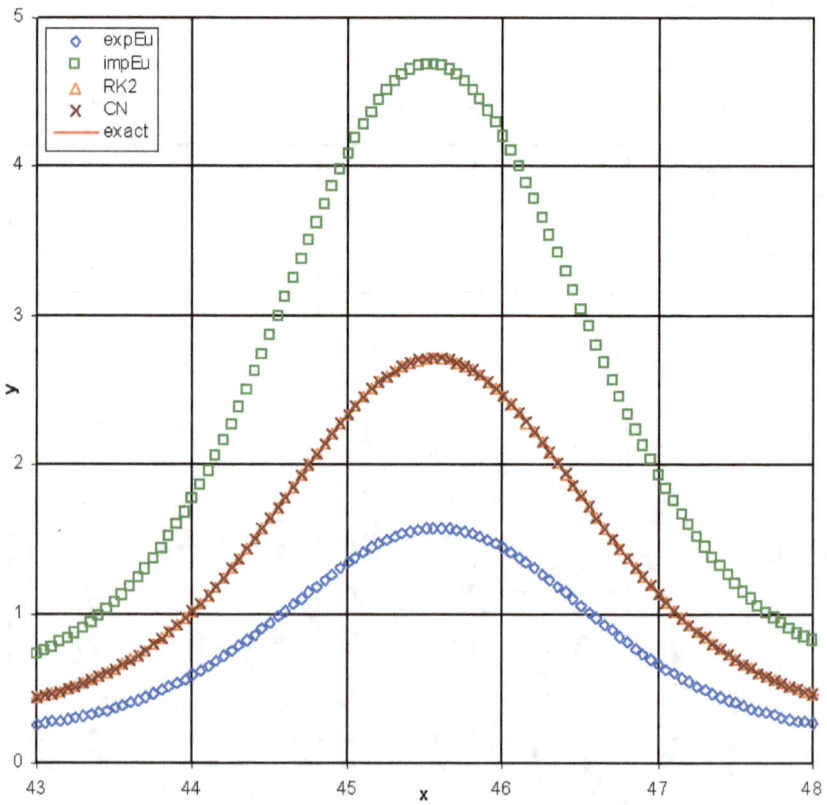

Figure 23. Exploded View of First Problem

Problem Two

The second problem we will consider with this same code and four methods is given by the following ODE:

$$\frac{dy}{dx} = \sin(y) \tag{16.7}$$

The analytical solution is:

$$y = \arctan\left(\frac{2e^x}{1+e^{2x}}, \frac{1-e^{2x}}{1+e^{2x}}\right) \tag{16.8}$$

The numerical solutions are shown in this next figure:

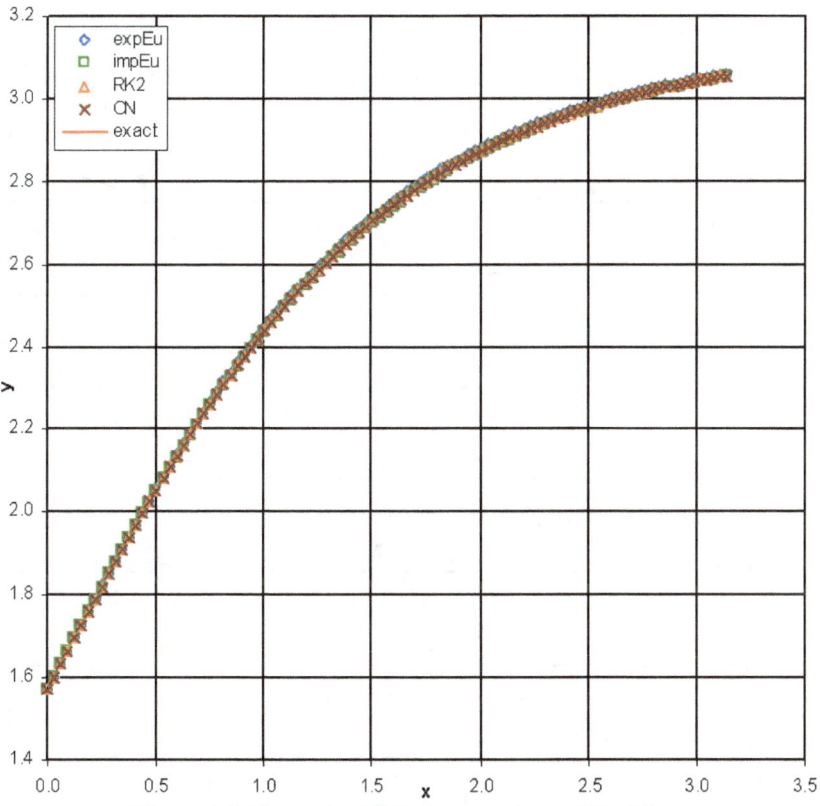

Figure 24. Numerical Solutions to Second Problem

All four solutions are on top of each other and continue on indefinitely in this same manner, indicating that it doesn't matter which method we use to solve this problem. Problems can be selected so as to illustrate a particular point that may not be a generalization.

Problem Three

The third problem is defined by the following ODE:

$$\frac{dy}{dx} = \frac{x^2}{y} \qquad (16.9)$$

The analytical solution is:

$$y = \sqrt{1 + \frac{2x^3}{6}} \qquad (16.10)$$

The numerical solutions are shown in this next figure:

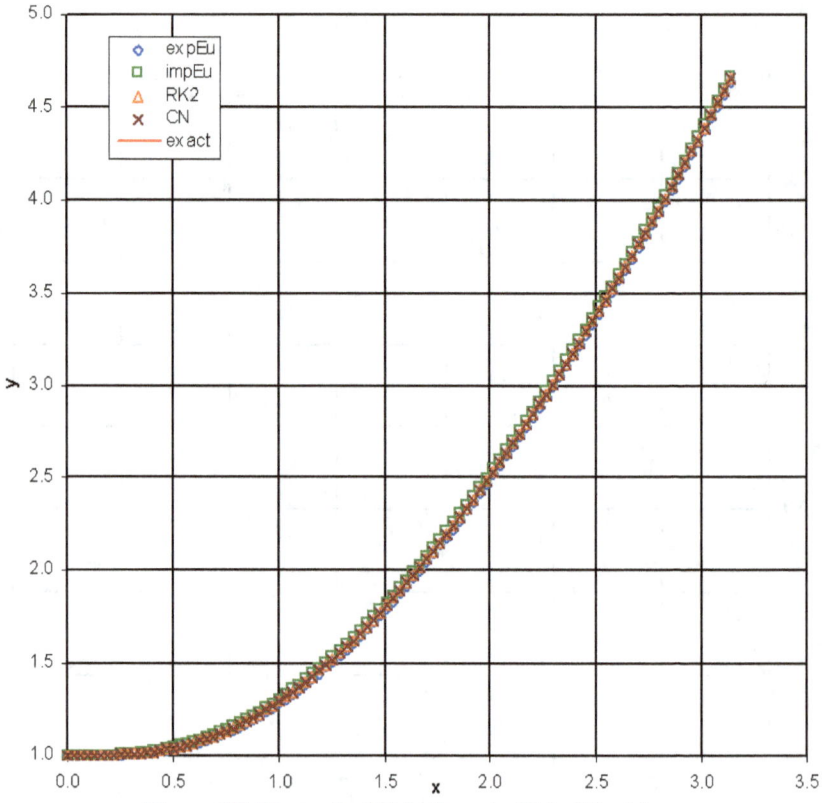

Figure 25. Numerical Solutions to Third Problem

In spite of the first two problems involving trigonometric functions and the third not, the shape of the second and third problems, which have entirely different analytical solutions, exhibit much the same behavior in that it doesn't matter which method is used.

Problem Four

The fourth problem is defined by the following ODE:

$$\frac{dy}{dx} = x\sin(x) \tag{16.11}$$

The analytical solution is:

$$y = \sin(x) - x\cos(x) \tag{16.12}$$

The numerical solutions are shown in this next figure:

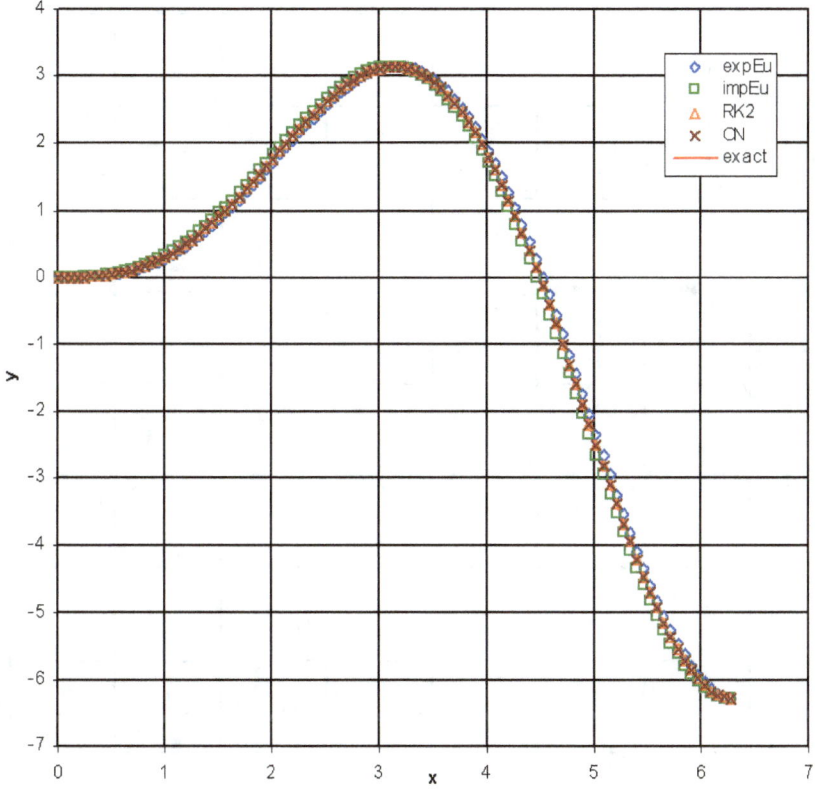

Figure 26. Numerical Solutions to Fourth Problem

Again and even with only 100 steps, it doesn't seem to matter which algorithm we choose. How can we be sure when we don't know the analytical solution? Divide the step size by 2 and see if it makes an appreciable difference. If it does, divide by 2 again. If it still does, try a more robust method.

<u>Problem Five</u>

The fifth problem is defined by the following ODE:

$$\frac{dy}{dx} = x^2 \cos(x) \tag{16.13}$$

The analytical solution is:

$$y = (x^2 - 2)\sin(x) + 2x\cos(x) \tag{16.14}$$

The numerical solutions are shown in this next figure:

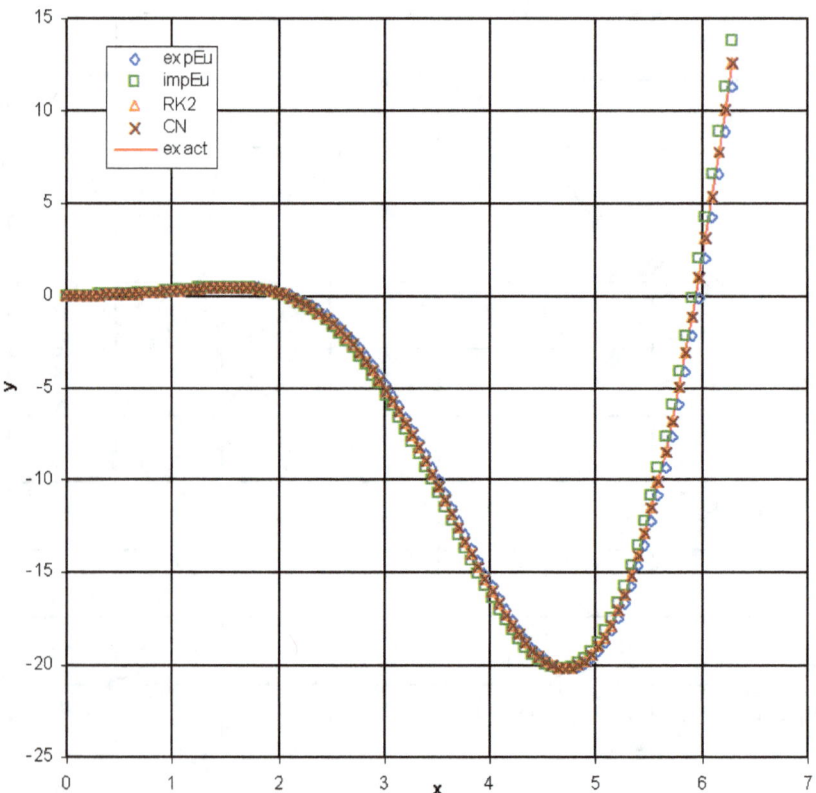

Figure 27. Numerical Solutions to Fifth Problem

Here we see some difference for x>5 with only 100 steps.

Decreasing the step size by a factor of two (or twice the number of steps) brings the results together, as illustrated in this next figure:

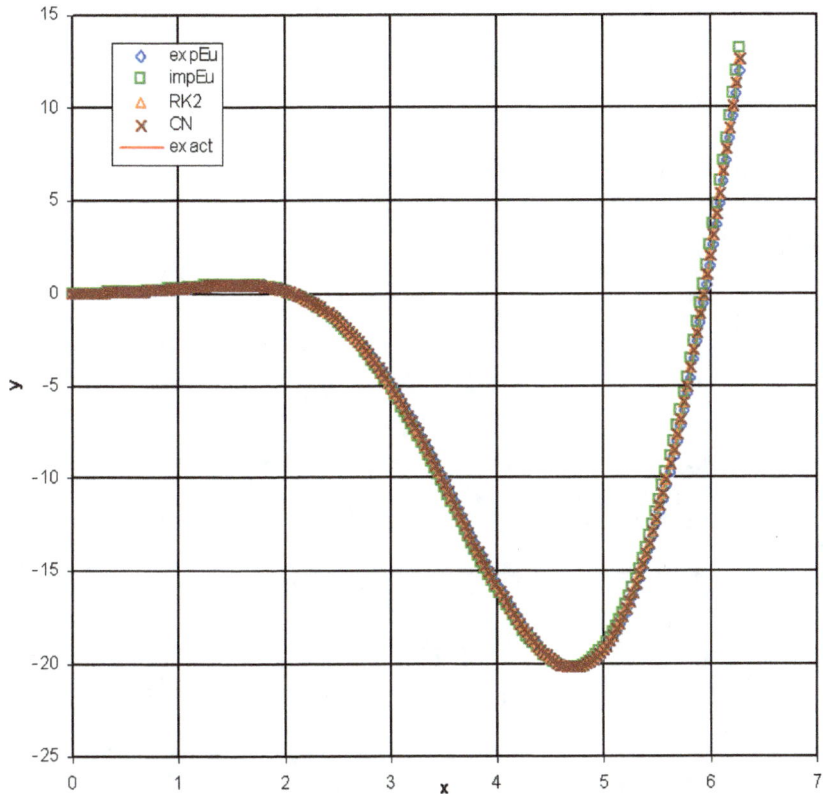

Figure 28. Numerical Solutions to Fifth Problem (with h/2)

In summary, use robust methods and check your results. Begin with large steps but check progressively smaller ones. Don't just assume but verify what you read online.

Appendix A. Instructions

Intel™ processors are capable of handling a considerable number of different instructions. We will only consider the most common here. It is vital that the efficient programmer understand what the chips can do in order to write optimal code. The following is a partial list of the most common instructions.

Table A1. Integer Arithmetic Instructions

instruction	ticks	action
ABS	2	absolute value
ADC	2	add with carry
ADD	3	unsigned add
AND	1	logical and
DEC	1	decrement
DIV	90	unsigned divide
IDIV	90	signed divide
IMUL	8	integer multiply
INC	1	increment
MUL	8	unsigned multiply
NEG	1	negative
NOT	1	logical not
OR	1	logical or
ROL	1	rotate left
ROR	1	rotate right
SAL	1	shift arithmetic left
SAR	1	shift arithmetic right
SBB	2	subtract with borrow
SHL	1	unsigned shift left
SHR	1	unsigned shift right
SUB	3	unsigned subtract
XOR	1	logical xor

The "tick count" in this table is an indicator of the approximate number of time steps (clock ticks) required to accomplish this task. This varies from one processor to another, even in the same family of Intel™ processors. Even if it doesn't exactly match every occurrence, it does serve as a relative indicator of how long these instructions take and why we might want to use one over the other.

As we will consider at more depth in Appendix B, there is a distinction between signed and unsigned integers. Note the separate instructions above (e.g., DIV/IDIV and MUL/IMUL) for signed and unsigned integers. While we most often use signed integers in calculations, all addresses (memory locations) are unsigned (there is no -3 memory block) so that both are necessary. Some very old processors (e.g., mainframes and mini-computers) didn't provide separate instructions, requiring additional code and memory to handle signs, carry, and borrow. This was a big plus for Intel™ processors when they were first introduced.

The separate shift and rotate instructions enable convenient management of the sign, carry, and borrow flags. Shift or rotate left 1 bit is equivalent to multiplying by 2. Shift or rotate right 1 bit is equivalent to dividing by 2. For Intel™ processors newer than the 80186, an integer number of shifts or rotations can be specified. On the 8086, this was only possible using the loop counter (CL, CX, ECX, or RCX register). As double precision floating-point values are 64-bit (8 BYTEs), the address increment is multiplied by 8. A simple and quick way of accomplishing this for a 32-bit array is:

```
SHL EAX,3
```

When we get into pre-processors we will see that the 8-BYTE increment in a double precision floating-point array can be accomplished as follows:

```
FLD QWORD PTR[EDX+ECX*8]
```

This means load a quad-WORD (8-BYTE) value onto the FPU stack at the address EDX+ECX*8. EDX will be the start of the array and ECX will be the index (as in x[i]). The pre-processor will multiply ECX by 8, add it to EDX, put it in a temporary register and pass the following to the main processor:

```
FLD QWORD PTR[temp]
```

The multiply and add will be performed by the pre-processor so that the effective timing will be that associated with the modified command. Adding a pre-processor greatly increased the effective speed of Intel™ processors.

Table A2. Address Instructions

instruction	ticks	action
LDS	1	load DS
LES	1	load ES
LEA	2	load effective address

The DS (data segment) and ES (extra segment) registers are used in 16-bit mode to address blocks of memory. EDS and EES are used in 32-bit mode. The instructions (LDS and LES) copy (load) a segment address from some location or operand into one of those two registers. The LEA instruction is more versatile and is used to copy (load) this same information into some other register. As we discuss in Appendix B, these registers are essential to accessing memory and so these instructions will appear many times in any code. Understanding which makes best use of resources and when is part of the optimization process, which we will illustrate by way of examples throughout the text.

Table A3. Loop Instructions

instruction	ticks	action
REP	n	repeat
LOOP	n	loop

These two instructions (repeat and loop) facilitate repetitive instructions. The REP instruction precedes and modifies a limited number of specific instructions, for example: repeat move BYTEs, as we shall see in the next grouping. The LOOP instruction is linked to the CX, ECX, or RCX registers, which must be loaded before executing this instruction. The LOOP instruction is also tied to a specific location within the code.

Table A4. Move Instructions

instruction	ticks	action
MOV	1	move
MOVSB	1	move sequential BYTE
MOVSW	1	move sequential WORD
MOVSD	1	move sequential DWORD

Move instructions must have a source and a destination, either explicit or implied. The qualifier (B/W/D/Q) indicates the size of the items to be moved (BYTE, WORD, double WORD, or quadruple WORD). These can be combined with the REP instruction, which presumes the loop counter (CX, ECX, or RCX) and also the source index (SI/ESI) and destination (DI/EDI).

Table A5. Calling and Returning Instructions

instruction	ticks	action
CALL	2+	jump to a procedure
RET	2+	return from a procedure

The CALL and RET instructions accomplish just that: jumping to and returning from a procedure. This action requires several steps, including at the very least, pushing the address where execution is to resume upon completion on the stack and jumping to the beginning of the procedure. The "stack" (a devoted block of memory) is necessary for this to work. Intel™ processors are "stack machines" that is, they use a *stack* of memory to save information (including addresses), which works like a cafeteria tray dispenser (last on, first off).

Before getting my first PC, I had to work with a processor that had no stack. When it was ready to jump into a procedure, it first stored the returning address at top of the procedure, then jumped just after that location. To return, it performed an indirect jump on the location stored at the beginning of the procedure. Of course, this means you could never have a reentrant procedure, such as qsort. Working with a stack machine is a huge benefit with Intel™ processors.

Table A6. Stack Instructions

instruction	ticks	action
POP	2	push on stack
PUSH	2	pop off stack

These two instructions add to and remove from the dynamic stack memory area, which the processor assumes is in a particular location SS:SP in 16-bit mode or SS:ESP in 32-bit mode or SS:RSP in 64-bit mode. It is vital to understand that if you leave something on the stack or remove too many items, disaster will result. The stack does not know what's on it and there is no checking to be sure you have tidied up after your procedure or not. The only somewhat checked stack operations are overflow (exceeding the top) or underflow (exceeding the bottom).

Subroutines and Temporary Variables

It is assumed that you will provide your own temporary space for a function, for which you may use the stack, as long as you remove the items before leaving. This is why it is most efficient to have a single RETURN statement in a higher code language (e.g., C, FORTRAN, Pascal), as these compilers will insert the "clean up" code for each return—not that it makes execution slower, only that it makes for more instructions. The most efficient (smaller compiled object) way is to jump to a single RETURN statement at the bottom of a procedure.

If you use any of the common registers in your subroutine, it is also assumed that you will save and restore these, something like the following:

```
      enter function
         PUSH ECX
         PUSH ESI
         PUSH EDI
    perform various tasks
         POP EDI
         POP ESI
         POP ECX
      exit function
```

Note the last on/first off order of the stack.

Conditional Jumps

Conditional jumps are an integral part of most coding. The following table is a partial list of the various options. The conditions listed as above or below are unsigned comparisons; whereas, greater or less than are signed comparisons. The carry and overflow flags are essential in many operations and are a huge improvements over the processors I began working with in 1975. The time to execute these conditional jumps does change from one to the other and also depending on the processor generation. All are listed as requiring 1 clock tick in the table for simplicity.

Table A7. Conditional Jump Instructions

instruction	ticks	action
JA	1	jump if above
JAE	1	jump if above or equal to
JB	1	jump if below
JBE	1	jump if below or equal
JC	1	jump if carry
JE	1	jump if equal
JG	1	jump if greater than
JGE	1	jump if greater than or equal to
JL	1	jump if less than
JLE	1	jump if less than or equal to
JNC	1	jump if not carry
JNE	1	jump if not equal
JNO	1	jump if not overflow
JO	1	jump if overflow

Appendix B. Registers

Registers for the Intel™ processors are of differing types and sizes. Some are for general usage, while others have a specific purpose. Some can be used in more than one way, while others can only be used in a single way. For example, you can't perform multiply and divide operations using a *segment* register. You can access any one of the low BYTEs of the general-purpose registers (AX, BX, CX, DX) but not the addressing (DI, SI) or segment (ES, DS, SS) registers. The following is a partial list of the most commonly used registers for Intel™ processors:

Table B1. Registers

BYTE	WORD	DWORD	QWORD
AL	AX	EAX	RAX
AH	BX	EBX	RBX
BL	CX	ECX	RCX
BH	DX	EDX	RDX
CL	DI	EDI	RDI
CH	SI	ESI	RSI
DL	BP	EBP	RBP
DH	SP	ESP	RSP

The term *BYTE* refers to eight grouped bits. The term *WORD* refers to sixteen grouped bits or two grouped BYTEs. The term *DWORD* refers to a double WORD or two grouped WORDs or four grouped BYTEs or thirty-two grouped bits. The term *QWORD* refers to two grouped DWORDs or four grouped WORDs or eight grouped BYTEs or sixty-four grouped bits. The term *nibble* refers to a half-BYTE or four grouped bits.

The first eight BYTE-size registers comprise the first four WORD-size registers (AH:AL=AX, BH:BL=BX, CH:CL=CX, DH:DL=DX). AX comprises the low 8 bits of EAX, though there is no direct way (with most processors in this family) to access the high 8 bits of EAX. If such is required, the shift instruction is used, as in:

```
SHR EAX,8
```

It is presumed the SI/ESI/RSI register will be used when referring to the address of a source operand, while the DI/EDI/RDI register refers to the address of a destination operand. Earlier processors allowed only these addressing combinations. For example, the 8086 would accept the first, but not the second of the following two instructions:

```
MOV AX,ES:DI
MOV AX,ES:DX
```

More recent processors can handle the second instruction, but note that these encodings are slightly larger (because a qualifier is required) and do take slightly longer to perform (nominally, although the pre-processor can overcome this, resulting in no appreciable difference). Keep this in mind when using these instructions.

Note also that most compilers don't presume that EAX, EBX, ECX, and EDX will be preserved (pushed on the stack and then popped off), while they do presume that EDI, ESI, EBP, and ESP will be preserved. All compilers presume that ES, DS, and SS (the primary stack segment addresses) and also FS and GS (the extended segment registers) will be preserved. These last 5 registers (ES, DS, SS, FS, and GS) are different from the ones listed in Table B1, as their size depends on the current operating mode (i.e., 16-bit, 32-bit, or 64-bit).

Appendix C. The FPU

Introduction of the Floating Point Unit, designed specifically to handle real (non-integer) numbers was a *huge* step in computing. I remember well the days when most PCs came without one and what all I had to go through to provide software to others (mostly attorneys and managers) who didn't have one of these amazing devices (or the extra megabyte of memory, which was also extra).

The following is a partial list of the most frequently used floating-point instructions and the approximate timing in clock ticks.

Table C1. Common Floating-Point Instructions

instruction	ticks	action
FABS	1	absolute value
FADD	8	add
FCHS	1	change sign
FCOM	1	compare
FCOS	60	partial cosine
FDIV	120	divide
FLD	1	load
FLDZ	1	load zero
FMUL	8	multiply
FNSTSW	1	store status word
FPATAN	120	partial arc tangent
FPTAN	90	partial tangent
FSIN	60	partial sine
FSQRT	20	partial square root
FST	1	store
FSTP	1	store and pop

The term *partial* in the table above (as in partial tangent) indicates that this is only part of the task of calculating a sine, cosine, tangent, etc. You must perform several steps before and after in order to obtain what one usually thinks of for such a transcendental function.

The way floating-point operations are performed is as follows for adding two real numbers: 1) load the first number onto the FPU stack using the FLD instruction; 2) load the second number onto the FPU stack; 3) perform the addition using the FADD instruction; 4) store the result somewhere using the FST instruction; 5) clean up the stack. We never actually perform these 5 steps because there is on FPOP instruction. Instead, we combine the store and pop tasks using the FSTP instruction. We can also include the second operand in the FADD instruction so that x=x+y becomes:

```
          FLD  ES: QWORD PTR[ESI]
          FMUL ES: QWORD PTR[EDI]
          FSTP ES: QWORD PTR[ESI]
```

where x is located at ES:ESI and y is located at ES:EDI.

Push & Pop

There is no FPUSH or FPOP instruction, yet we must manage the FPU stack. This is accomplished with the FLD (puts something on the stack) and FSTP (stores something and pops the stack). Make no mistake about it, under- or over-flowing the FPU stack will crash your program. Also note that the size of the FPU stack varies with the processor model. Should you need to pop the FPU stack but don't want the value at the top, simply use the following:

```
FSTP ST(0)
```

which stores the result on top of itself (zero position on the stack) and then pops. You can also access other members of the FPU stack in this way, for example:

```
FMUL ST(1)
```

which multiplies ST(0) by ST(1).

80-Bit Integers

Most programmers don't realize that Intel™ FPUs can readily handle 80-bit integers and perform calculations with these at a much faster rate than the main processor. While this has become almost superfluous with 64-bit operating systems and code, it was a big deal in the days of 16-bit and 32-bit operating systems. Many 64-bit operations are not too taxing in 32-bit mode, but they were quite burdensome in 16-bit mode. For example, multiplies (MUL) using the AX and BX registers automatically overflow into the DX register, forming the DWORD DX:AX. Likewise, divides using the AX and BX registers automatically store the remainder in the DX register. Performing the equivalent operations while not operating in 64-bit mode is more complicated. Microsoft's 32-bit C compiler implemented these operations by inserting a function call.

Table C2. Common FPU Integer Instructions

instruction	ticks	action
FIADD	2	add integers
FICOMP	2	compare integers
FIDIV	8	divide integers
FIMUL	4	multiply integers
FISUB	2	subtract integers
FILD	1	load integer
FIST	1	store integer
FISTP	1	store integer and pop
FRNDINT	2	round to nearest integer

Not only do Intel™ FPUs natively operate with 80-bit integers, they also operate natively with 80-bit floating-point numbers, regardless of how they are represented within your code. This means that there is also a TBYTE, which is ten consecutive BYTEs or 80-bits.

Appendix D. Steam Properties in Assembler

The first continuous steam property formulation was published by Keenan, Keyes, Hill, and Moore in 1969[39]. This mathematically elegant approach never received the proper notoriety or usage, partly due to the lack of FPUs in the early days of computing. The piecemeal, discontinuous, but computationally faster approach of Meyer, McClintock, Silvestri, and Spencer, published two years earlier[40] and sanctioned by the American Society of Mechanical Engineers, eclipsed it. The piecemeal formulation necessarily contained discontinuities, which could cause thermodynamic cycle modeling software depending on these properties to stumble (mine, for example).

The KKHM approach began with a two-part expression for the Helmholtz Free Energy:

$$a = a_0(T) + RT(\ln \rho + \rho Q(T, \rho)) \tag{D.1}$$

The first part, a_0, is a function of temperature only. The second part, Q, is a function of temperature and density. This form inherently reduces to ideal gas behavior as the density approaches zero. The first part can be entirely derived from the constant volume specific heat at zero density, C_{V0}:

$$a_0(T) = \int \left(\int \frac{C_{V0}}{T} dT \right) dT + A_1 T + A_2 \tag{D.2}$$

Equation D.2 follows directly from integrating $a=u-Ts$ for an ideal gas. The two integrals ($du_0/dT=C_{V0}$ and $dS_0/dT=C_{V0}/T$) can be combined to form the single integral above. The two constants of integration complete the expression. The pressure follows from one of Maxwell's relationships:

$$p = -\left(\frac{\partial a}{\partial v}\right)_T = \rho^2 \left(\frac{\partial a}{\partial \rho}\right)_T \tag{D.3}$$

Substituting Equation D.1 into D.3 yields:

$$p = \rho RT \left[1 + \rho Q + \rho^2 \left(\frac{\partial Q}{\partial \rho}\right)_T \right] \tag{D.4}$$

KKHM first performed a regression on the critical isotherm vs. density, then crafted their series expansion of Q so as to reduce to this relationship when $T=T_C$. Linear least-squares was employed to obtain suitable coefficients, along

---

[39] Keenan, J. H., Keyes, F. G., Hill, P. G., and Moore, J. G., Steam Tables, John Wiley & Sons, Inc., 1969.

[40] Meyer, C. A., McClintock, R. B., Silvestri, G. J., and Spencer, R. C., Jr., Thermodynamic and Transport Properties of Steam, American Society of Mechanical Engineers, 1967.

with linear constraints to match select values, including u_0 and s_0 at the triple point as well as the maximum liquid density at 4°C. Their Appendix is quite informative I highly recommended reading it.

To overcome the greater computational effort, I encoded the KKHM steam properties entirely in assembler, first for the HP-1000 minicomputer and later adapted to the Intel™ 8087. My entire original code (both FORTRAN and assembler) can be found in the online archive in the folder examples\KKHM. A sample listing follows:

```
L200:   MOV     SI,OFFSET T0            ;IF(T.EQ.T0) GO TO 300
        FLD     CS:DWORD PTR[SI]
        LES     DI,[BP+22]
        FLD     ES:DWORD PTR[DI]
        FST     CS:DWORD PTR[SI]        ;T0=T
        FSUBP   ST(1),ST(0)
        CALL    FTEST
        FSTP    ST(0)
        JNE     L201
        JMP     L300
L201:   MOV     DI,OFFSET T0            ;TAU=1800./(T+459.67)
        FLD     CS:DWORD PTR[DI]
        MOV     DI,OFFSET DD459
        FADD    CS:DWORD PTR[DI]
        MOV     DI,OFFSET DD1800
        FLD     CS:DWORD PTR[DI]
        FXCH    ST(1)
        FDIVP   ST(1),ST(0)
        MOV     DI,OFFSET TAU
        FST     CS:DWORD PTR[DI]
        FLD1
        FDIV    ST(0),ST(1)             ;OTAU=1./TAU
        MOV     DI,OFFSET OTAU
        FSTP    CS:DWORD PTR[DI]
        FLD     ST(0)                   ;T00=TAU/1000.
        MOV     DI,OFFSET DD1000
        FDIV    CS:DWORD PTR[DI]
        MOV     DI,OFFSET T00
        FST     CS:DWORD PTR[DI]
        FLDLN2                          ;TL=-ALOG(T00)
        FXCH    ST(1)
        FYL2X
        FCHS
        MOV     DI,OFFSET TL
```

While the speed of steam properties is no longer a concern with all current Intel™ processors having built-in FPUs, that doesn't mean that there won't be similar challenges in the future, which can also be overcome by carefully crafting specialized code to best utilize available resources, as was done here.

Appendix E. Moist Air Properties in Assembler

Steam properties weren't the first challenge that I was able to overcome by resorting to assembler. Before switching from one application to another became standard with all modern operating systems, if calculations were required while composing or editing a document, this necessitated exiting one and launching the other application unless you had two computers. Someone created a popup calculator that was quite useful so I created a popup program to calculate moist air properties and then another to calculate steam properties, which were even more convenient than looking up values in a book. Such popup programs were called TSRs (terminate and stay resident).

TSRs could only be written in assembler. Implementing properties required not only encoding the properties themselves but also writing the results as numbers in boxes on the screen, as print() does not exist in assembler. The entire code, which can be found in the folder examples\POPSYCH is only 6732 bytes. Though I wrote it in 1982, it will still run on any 32-bit version of Windows™ if launched from a command prompt or on a 64-bit version in a virtual box.

```
POPSYCH/V1.3: psychrometrics by Dudley J. Benton
this copy licensed to:
dry-bulb      15.6°C        wet-bulb      15.6°C
dew-point     15.6°C        rel. hum.    100.0%
abs. hum.    .01109         sat. hum.    .01109
enthalpy     34.36 J/gm     sat. ent.    34.36 J/gm
density      1.215 kg/m^3   volume       .83221 m^3/kg
elevation    0 m            pressure     .10135 MPa

           press tab to change input field
         press Home/End to change function
    press ↑↓ to increase/decrease value in input field
    press PgUp/Dn increase/decrease in larger increment
       press ctrl-PgUp/Dn for still larger increments
    press U to swap English/SI units         Esc to exit
```

While this application is of some historical interest, it also illustrates that carefully crafted code can have a very long lifetime (in this case 40 years), making it well worth the investment of your time to do it right the first time. I have recycled the underlying (very efficient) code, which calculates moist air properties many times, including a widely-used Excel Add-In.

Appendix F. Procedure Level Timing

While you can get function timing in FORTRAN by using calls to the library before and after executing each procedure of interest:

```
REAL*8 T1,T2
CALL CPU_TIME(T1)
do something tedious...
CALL CPU_TIME(T2)
WRITE(*,*)'seconds=',T2-T1
```

and by getting the timer tick and rate from the Windows™ O/S in C with:

```
extern int __stdcall QueryPerformanceFrequency(__int64*);
extern int __stdcall QueryPerformanceCounter(__int64*);
 __int64 rate,t1,t2;
QueryPerformanceFrequency(&rate);
QueryPerformanceCounter(&t1);
do something tedious...=
QueryPerformanceCounter(&t2);
printf("seconds=%6.4lf\n",(t2-t1)/((double)rate));
```

it can be quite revealing (and also convenient) to have the compiler do this for you. When last I checked, there are some very expensive FORTRAN and C compilers (e.g., Intel™) that provide this important information. This especially makes sense for Intel™ to provide such a capability so as to better utilize their marvelous processors.

If you're on a tight budget (like me, unwilling to spend a cent on anything that isn't absolutely necessary), there is another option. Walter Bright wrote the first single-pass C++ compiler, which was called Zortech. He went to work for Symantec, who sold it for several years under their brand name, but found they couldn't make any money, so they dropped it. A similar sad story can be told for the various FORTRAN compilers. Walter Bright now gives this wonderful tool away and you can get it from his website:

https://www.digitalmars.com/

Before you dismiss some of the old packages that are available at this site, consider that these (like the runtime library source code and the x32 extender) contain some very interesting code from random number generation to memory manipulation to manual process switching that might be useful for other tasks.

To activate function-level timing, simply run any one of Walter Bright's compilers with the –gt switch, run the program, and look for the output file named trace.log. In this you will find how many times each function was called and by what and how long it took by itself as well as including the functions that it called.

Appendix G. Speed Test

While there are many speed tests available online, these may not come with the source code and they may not focus on crunching numbers. You will find such a program (howfast.c) in the examples\howfast folder of the online archive accompanying this text at the link shown below the Preface. It is organized to be compiled with the VisualStudio™ C compiler. Some typical sections are listed below, this particular one for integer instructions:

```
int Instructions()
  {
  w+=3;x-=5;y*=7;z/=9;
  w-=3;x+=5;y/=7;z*=9;
  w+=3;x-=5;y*=7;z/=9;
  w-=3;x+=5;y/=7;z*=9;
  w+=3;x-=5;y*=7;z/=9;
  w-=3;x+=5;y/=7;z*=9;
```

and this one for floating-point instructions:

```
#define PI    3.14159265358979323846
#define LOG2  0.30102999566398119521
#define LN2   0.69314718055994530941 72321
#define LOG2T 3.32192809488736234787
#define LOG2E 1.44269504088896 34074
int FloatingPoint()
  {
  W+=PI;X-=LOG2;Y*=LOG2T;Z/=LOG2E;
  W-=PI;X+=LOG2;Y/=LOG2T;Z*=LOG2E;
  W+=PI;X-=LOG2;Y*=LOG2T;Z/=LOG2E;
  W-=PI;X+=LOG2;Y/=LOG2T;Z*=LOG2E;
```

The results for an Intel™ 2.19 GHz Centrino™ processor are:

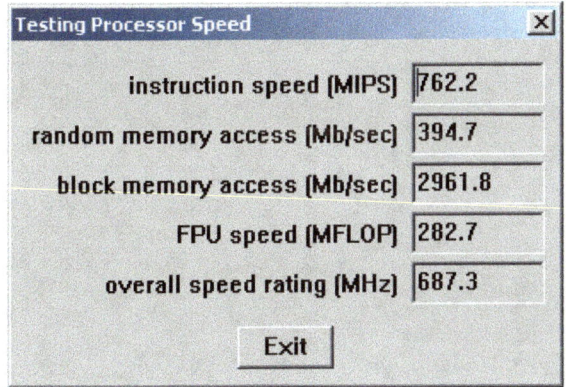

The results for an Intel™ 2.29 GHz Core i5™ are:

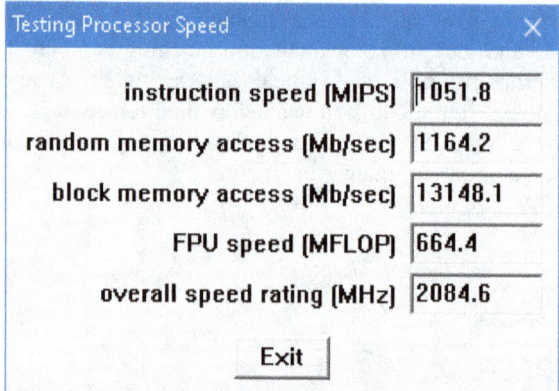

The i5 is definitely faster but the FPU is only about 2.4× faster, which is the part I most care about. The MIPS are only 1.4× faster. I really don't care about block memory access or that it's 4.4× faster. Perhaps this would be of interest if I sat around all day watching YouTube™ videos, but I don't. The 2.19 GHz processor works out to about 0.69 GIPS (giga instructions per second) and the 2.29 GHz processor works out to about 2.08 GIPS, which is a relative improvement and does reveal the even more advanced pre-processor and efficient architecture.

also by D. James Benton

3D Articulation: Using OpenGL, ISBN-9798596362480, Amazon, 2021 (book 3 in the 3D series).

3D Models in Motion Using OpenGL, ISBN-9798652987701, Amazon, 2020 (book 2 in the 3D series.

3D Rendering in Windows: How to display three-dimensional objects in Windows with and without OpenGL, ISBN-9781520339610, Amazon, 2016 (book 1 in the 3D series).

A Synergy of Short Stories: The whole may be greater than the sum of the parts, ISBN-9781520340319, Amazon, 2016.

Azeotropes: Behavior and Application, ISBN-9798609748997, Amazon, 2020.

bat-Elohim: Book 3 in the Little Star Trilogy, ISBN-9781686148682, Amazon, 2019.

Boilers: Performance and Testing, ISBN: 9798789062517, Amazon 2021.

Combined 3D Rendering Series: 3D Rendering in Windows®, 3D Models in Motion, and 3D Articulation, ISBN-9798484417032, Amazon, 2021.

Complex Variables: Practical Applications, ISBN-9781794250437, Amazon, 2019.

Compression & Encryption: Algorithms & Software, ISBN-9781081008826, Amazon, 2019.

Computational Fluid Dynamics: an Overview of Methods, ISBN-9781672393775, Amazon, 2019.

Computer Simulation of Power Systems: Programming Strategies and Practical Examples, ISBN-9781696218184, Amazon, 2019.

Contaminant Transport: A Numerical Approach, ISBN-9798461733216, Amazon, 2021.

Curve-Fitting: The Science and Art of Approximation, ISBN-9781520339542, Amazon, 2016.

Death by Tie: It was the best of ties. It was the worst of ties. It's what got him killed., ISBN-9798398745931, Amazon, 2023.

Differential Equations: Numerical Methods for Solving, ISBN-9781983004162, Amazon, 2018.

Equations of State: A Graphical Comparison, ISBN-9798843139520, Amazon, 2022.

Evaporative Cooling: The Science of Beating the Heat, ISBN-9781520913346, Amazon, 2017.

Forecasting: Extrapolation and Projection, ISBN-9798394019494, Amazon 2023.

Heat Engines: Thermodynamics, Cycles, & Performance Curves, ISBN-9798486886836, Amazon, 2021.

Heat Exchangers: Performance Prediction & Evaluation, ISBN-9781973589327, Amazon, 2017.

Heat Recovery Steam Generators: Thermal Design and Testing, ISBN-9781691029365, Amazon, 2019.

Heat Transfer: Heat Exchangers, Heat Recovery Steam Generators, & Cooling Towers, ISBN-9798487417831, Amazon, 2021.

Heat Transfer Examples: Practical Problems Solved, ISBN-9798390610763, Amazon, 2023.
The Kick-Start Murders: Visualize revenge, ISBN-9798759083375, Amazon, 2021.
Jamie2: Innocence is easily lost and cannot be restored, ISBN-9781520339375, Amazon, 2016-18.
Kyle Cooper Mysteries: Kick Start, Monte Carlo, and Waterfront Murders, ISBN-9798829365943, Amazon, 2022.
The Last Seraph: Sequel to Little Star, ISBN-9781726802253, Amazon, 2018.
Little Star: God doesn't do things the way we expect Him to. He's better than that! ISBN-9781520338903, Amazon, 2015-17.
Living Math: Seeing mathematics in every day life (and appreciating it more too), ISBN-9781520336992, Amazon, 2016.
Lost Cause: If only history could be changed..., ISBN-9781521173770, Amazon, 2017.
Mass Transfer: Diffusion & Convection, ISBN-9798702403106, Amazon, 2021.
Mill Town Destiny: The Hand of Providence brought them together to rescue the mill, the town, and each other, ISBN-9781520864679, Amazon, 2017.
Monte Carlo Murders: Who Killed Who and Why, ISBN-9798829341848, Amazon, 2022.
Monte Carlo Simulation: The Art of Random Process Characterization, ISBN-9781980577874, Amazon, 2018.
Nonlinear Equations: Numerical Methods for Solving, ISBN-9781717767318, Amazon, 2018.
Numerical Calculus: Differentiation and Integration, ISBN-9781980680901, Amazon, 2018.
Numerical Methods: Nonlinear Equations, Numerical Calculus, & Differential Equations, ISBN-9798486246845, Amazon, 2021.
Orthogonal Functions: The Many Uses of, ISBN-9781719876162, Amazon, 2018.
Overwhelming Evidence: A Pilgrimage, ISBN-9798515642211, Amazon, 2021.
Particle Tracking: Computational Strategies and Diverse Examples, ISBN-9781692512651, Amazon, 2019.
Plumes: Delineation & Transport, ISBN-9781702292771, Amazon, 2019.
Power Plant Performance Curves: for Testing and Dispatch, ISBN-9798640192698, Amazon, 2020.
Practical Linear Algebra: Principles & Software, ISBN-9798860910584, Amazon, 2023.
Props, Fans, & Pumps: Design & Performance, ISBN-9798645391195, Amazon, 2020.
Remediation: Contaminant Transport, Particle Tracking, & Plumes, ISBN-9798485651190, Amazon, 2021.
ROFL: Rolling on the Floor Laughing, ISBN-9781973300007, Amazon, 2017.
Seminole Rain: You don't choose destiny. It chooses you, ISBN-9798668502196, Amazon, 2020.
Septillionth: 1 in 10^{24}, ISBN-9798410762472, Amazon, 2022.

Software Development: Targeted Applications, ISBN-9798850653989, Amazon, 2023.

Software Recipes: Proven Tools, ISBN-9798815229556, Amazon, 2022.

Steam 2020: to 150 GPa and 6000 K, ISBN-9798634643830, Amazon, 2020.

Thermochemical Reactions: Numerical Solutions, ISBN-9781073417872, Amazon, 2019.

Thermodynamic and Transport Properties of Fluids, ISBN-9781092120845, Amazon, 2019.

Thermodynamic Cycles: Effective Modeling Strategies for Software Development, ISBN-9781070934372, Amazon, 2019.

Thermodynamics - Theory & Practice: The science of energy and power, ISBN-9781520339795, Amazon, 2016.

Version-Independent Programming: Code Development Guidelines for the Windows® Operating System, ISBN-9781520339146, Amazon, 2016.

The Waterfront Murders: As you sow, so shall you reap, ISBN-9798611314500, Amazon, 2020.

Weather Data: Where To Get It and How To Process It, ISBN-9798868037894, Amazon, 2023.